Matthew Jackson

The Retirement Dreammaker

Master the Art of Retirement Abundance

In honor of all who have inspired and encouraged for good.

CONTENTS

HOW TO TAKE ACTION

FULLFILLMENT AND WHY

RETIREMENT REVOLUTION

INTRODUCTION

> "You are never too old to dream a new dream."
> ~ C.S. Lewis

Ever since I can remember, I've had my head in the clouds. I've always dreamed of what could be possible in the future. I was no different than any other kid in this respect. When we are young, we all dream about what we want our "world" to look like.

I would dream about taking adventures in nature, exploring the world, and being Peter Pan or Superman. As I got older, I would dream about becoming a state champion gymnast, going to college, becoming a national champion gymnast, having a beautiful, loving wife, and driving my dream car. I really love cars.

After college, I would dream about owning my own business, helping people, making a difference in others' lives, finding a soul mate, and achieving financial success. I chased those dreams with everything I had: all of my discipline, determination, and hope.

As I started my own businesses, found my soul mate, and achieved financial success, my dreams became goals to accomplish. I added each accomplishment to the list, and as each goal was checked off, I did what most people do. I thought of the next challenge to cross off the list. For the better part of 15 years, I chased the feeling of being full, marking one personal or business challenge after the other, always chasing, always pursuing.

Even though I was checking off my goals, one by one, I always kept my deepest dream, of helping people in a meaningful way, alive in my heart. However, securing financial freedom and accomplishing business milestones, admittedly, were most important in my younger years. Painful life experiences, including business challenges and personal loss, forced me to give up what I was truly passionate about. I "had to do what I had to do" to be responsible for my family and for myself.

Does this sound familiar? Has this happened to you? I believe this has happened to a lot of us. Our dreams get put on the hold because of the daily challenges of everyday life. We somehow get fooled into needing the bigger bank account, the better car, a bigger house, and an endless list of "necessities" because "life" tells us that's what we should be doing.

I found myself ignoring my heart and listening to my head, even though my heart was still telling me that I wasn't following my true passions. The more I ignored my heart, the easier it was to justify what I was doing. It didn't matter whether I was doing it out of necessity or because my ego was in control.

Looking back, I see how my dreams became goals, and my goals became milestones. The list of my achievements began to internally define me. They became the terms I would use to define myself.

I'm grateful for the goals I've accomplished and the milestones I've checked off. My list isn't done. I've got more to do. I'm dreaming new dreams and following my heart. Life is an evolution, not an event. I'm evolving in every way I can: personally, professionally, and spiritually.

It's my sincerest wish that you find the tools in this book useful to help you evolve. We all deserve to get the most we can out of life. You're never too old to dream a new dream.

FORWARD

This is not your typical retirement planning book. The design layout is the exact opposite of almost all of the books I've read on retirement planning. Inspiration for this book came to me in November of 2016. My mother, Irene R. Lawler, had passed just a few weeks earlier, and I was on a personal retreat recovering from the emotional exhaustion of the last year's events.

Sitting on the beach reflecting on the past year's loss of both of our family dogs, my uncle, and my mother, I was trying to find inspiration to move on to a better life. The compounded pain of those losses had me emotionally exhausted, but not defeated.

I learned a lot in that year about gratitude, love, strength, relationships, and money. The experience put me at the tipping point of my life. During the years prior to 2016, I had been slowly, but methodically, working on my personal and professional growth and development.

Most of 2016, I found myself simply maintaining the positive thoughts, beliefs and habits I had developed to that point, rather than building on them. It was through enduring the personal losses of 2016 that gratitude for the work I had done on myself prior hit an all-time high for me. The improvements I had made in my thinking over the years helped me to take the experiences of 2016 and turn them into a positive.

You may be surprised that I only dedicate a small portion of this book to financial advice. Make no mistake: the concepts I'm sharing with you are very powerful, even though I'm not dedicating an entire book to them. If you do nothing more than read and apply those chapters to your life, you will be much better off financially. The tips I'm sharing with you are the closely guarded secrets of the investment industry, who wants to suck the growth and performance out of your retirement accounts for their financial gain. The chapters will help you avoid the cleverly disguised pitfalls of people and principles that may significantly decrease your chances for a stable, fulfilling retirement.

Few things make me happier than being able to expose the pitfalls of retirement saving and investing, which prevent so many from having an extraordinary opportunity for financial and personal happiness. I've always been a champion of the underdog, and it seems that in the game of investing, saving, and planning for retirement we, the Main Street investors, are the underdog. I've learned the game is hideously stacked against the trusting investor who doesn't take the time to learn some very simple principles about investing. Hint. Hint. Your stockbroker doesn't want you to learn them either. I'll be teaching you the same principles I teach my private clients, ideas that have successfully helped them avoid retirement-eroding pitfalls.

These are very basic and simple principles that will make you want to smack yourself in the head when you read them. They will make you wonder why no one has taken the time to share them with you and why good people continue to run head first into these traps. Please don't be the person who learns about a better way of investing but does nothing about it. Knowledge with no action will only perpetuate the past. Take action! There are good people who can help you. You just need to know how to find them in your community. I will be providing a checklist on www.TheRetirementDreammaker.com to help you find people and organizations who can help you find the best opportunities for financial success and retirement fulfillment.

Money is not the only source of happiness in our lives, but it can be a significant barrier to being true to ourselves, pursuing our passions, helping others, and finding stability. Don't believe that money is a barrier to happiness? Here are a few examples of how money can be a barrier in our lives.

- You want to take a fitness class with your friends. It costs $60 per month. You don't have enough room in your budget. You can't go.

- You would like to start a business you're passionate about, and the investment to get started is $50,000. You don't have enough cash, and your credit isn't good enough. There is no business to start.

- Your long-time friends are taking a vacation and invite you to go. The trip costs $15,000, but you just replaced your furnace. No vacation for you.

- You have lived in your home for 30 years, and your spouse has an eye on your dream retirement home in your dream retirement location. You didn't get good investment advice, and your retirement savings are lagging. Good luck moving into your dream home in your dream location.

If you're reading this book and feeling like you've already lost too much time to make an impact on what has already happened up to this point in your retirement investing plan, don't fall for this trap. It's not too late, and the recommendations I'm sharing may have a dramatic impact going forward.

Think of it this way: if you're on a road trip and get lost after a wrong turn, you don't keep going the wrong direction. You stop the car. You read your map and get reoriented with your location. You take the next exit and get back to heading in the right direction. Honestly, your retirement investing direction is no different. It's never too late to change direction!

GET ON THE RIGHT PATH!

The second reason I'm writing this book is because I want all my readers to find the best opportunities for a fulfilling retirement. Selfishly, I want to die a happy death. Not a premature death. I'm not racing to get to the pearly gates. When it's my time to go to the other side, I don't want to have regrets for things I didn't do, the person I wasn't, or the adventures I waited to do.

Through coaching sports and retirement planning, I've always loved inspiring people to do more than they thought they could ever manage. There is no better feeling than seeing a person's life become better through your inspiration. We are in a wonderful place in time that we get to shape exactly what retirement is for us. No other generation has been better positioned to take advantage of what I refer to as the "triangle of success" in retirement.

Many of the people I've interviewed over the years are scared and apprehensive to talk about what the future holds for them in retirement. There is a lot of uncertainty about what retirement will look like. What will be done with all of the "free time"? How will being with the spouse full-time play out? How to manage finances? The pages that follow are designed to take those fears away and give you more certainty of what the future can hold for you, through other retirees' experiences. We can learn from them, avoid common mistakes, and streamline our ability for the most possible success and fulfillment in retirement. Together, we can reshape what retirement is!

> We don't know what we don't know.

As a Brazilian jiu-jitsu practitioner, I'm constantly reminded of this when I'm caught in a stranglehold or a joint lock. Countless times, I've been caught in unfamiliar positions, not able to move. When I ask my training partner how I got caught in the losing position and how to escape, the answers are often ridiculously obvious. The lesson can only be chalked up to experience of not knowing what we don't know.

Retirement is a new event for everyone, and I see people falling into the same strangleholds every day. It's frustrating to see the same events cause the same pain in peoples' lives. This book can't help you avoid all of the challenges of retirement, but it can be a great resource of how to identify and navigate through them. If the pages in this book represent the only place that you can get the truth about the challenges facing you in retirement, then I've accomplished a goal of mine.

Why not consult a playbook that you can use to your advantage? I could have been spared a lot of pain in life, in general, if someone would have handed me a playbook that spelled out, "If you'd like to increase your chances for success and streamline your growth, avoid these painful mistakes." More important, here are the signs to look out for if you are beginning to head down the incorrect path, and here are the keys to the escape from life's strangleholds.

You don't have to be the person who learns the hard way about retirement traps. You can be the person to dance around the traps. You can rediscover, reinvent, and reconnect with yourself, your spouse, your family, and your community with ease and stability. You are in the "triangle of success" in your life! You will see you have all of the tools you need and you can easily use them to your advantage.

When you're done with this book, you can expect to be able to use it as a source of empowerment and inspiration. There are countless books on financial success in retirement, but very few address the emotional and spiritual success paths in retirement. You will have tools to empower you to grow in ways you didn't think possible, reshape your life, do the things you've delayed doing, and be the person you have always wanted to be.

Make no mistake, it is no easy task reshaping and building a new life in retirement. You're going to have many obstacles in your way. When you begin reshaping your life, you can expect to hear your family and friends tell you your acting different or crazy. Stay the course! You may feel the pull of complacency and the tendencies to stay in your old habits. Stay the course! Family and friends may be jealous of your courage and discipline to change and don't like seeing you out of their comfort zone. Stay the course! The media is going to keep showing you images of what your retirement should look like, not the retirement you want to live. Stay the course! Your stockbroker may not like the way you're funding the pursuit of your dreams. Stay the course! Negative thoughts may creep into your brain, discouraging your success and growth. Stay the course! You may have a health complication. To the best of your ability, stay the course!

Nothing worth having in life comes easy. If you live a life congruent to your true passions, and you have the comfort of a stable retirement structure, it can be much easier to work through the daily difficulties of growing. At times, it will seem as if every obstacle is being put in your way to stop your progress. Don't stop. Take a rest if you need to, but don't ever stop. It takes daily discipline, direction, and encouragement. I'm encouraging you to grow in ways you've always wanted, to do what you've always wanted, and to be the person you've always wanted to be. Break the mold, and go for it!

October 18th, 2016 Irene R. Lawler (age 69 years 17 days) passed to the other side.

CHAPTER 1
COURAGE AND DEDICATION

"Success is not final, failure is not fatal:
it is the courage to continue that counts."
~ Winston Churchill

Gymnastics built my confidence daily, helping me overcome my fears and showing me that I was capable of more than what logic would allow. It helped me to be resilient in the face of certain failure and injury, even though I sprained and strained most parts of my body and broke most of my fingers and toes, both of my ankles and wrists, and even my back! Seeing how far I could get was way more fulfilling than the pain of any injury.

One of the stories that stick out is: when I was a senior in college and my team was getting ready for a meet against another university, I was on the high-bar event practicing my dismounts. If you know nothing about men's gymnastics, just remember that the bar is nine feet off the ground. My dismount was a double lay-out (two flips in the air with your body as straight as a board). To be successful, you have to go around the bar as fast as humanly possible, let go of the bar at the exact right time, then fly a few feet higher than the bar and land six to ten feet away from the bar. (Did I mention that the bar is nine feet off the ground???)

To say getting off of the high bar is a bit scary is a total understatement for me. Although it was a freaking awesome feeling, it scared the living day lights out of me. The excitement I got from flipping off of the high bar had more to do with the relief that I landed safely, than the feeling of flying twelve to fourteen feet in the air, flipping multiple times and landing on my feet without moving an inch, all with perfect precision.

Honestly, there were a lot of times in practice when I flat chickened-out of letting go of the bar and would just hang on and go around one more time. It must have driven my coach crazy! I had done it so many times in practice that I had a pretty good reputation of not letting go of the bar, even though I had one of the highest and best dismounts on our team. The speed, height, and the fact that my feet were whizzing by that little aluminum bar, at seemingly light speed, were always in the back of my mind, testing my courage.

So there I was in practice, getting ready for our next meet. I pulled myself on top of the bar, casted to a handstand position and got going around the bar as fast as I could: one time, two times, then, at the exact moment I had to let go of the bar to fly eleven feet in the air and eight feet away from the bar… I miss it… by a millisecond. I catapult myself a few feet above the bar on my first flip. On the second flip, as I'm squeezing all of my muscles as tightly as I can to stay straight, I can feel I am too close to the bar. It's too late. I'm flying too fast to do anything about it.

I remember clenching my teeth, waiting for it to happen. I had held on too long for a split second, and I knew exactly what was going to happen. Time reduced to slow motion in anticipation of what I knew was coming. In an instant, on my second flip, on the way down to the ground, my shins hit the aluminum bar so hard that it catapulted me the entire opposite directions, slamming me on to the "crash" mat!
Wham!!!

Try to imagine how fast I was flipping to make both rotations before the ground. Now imagine how much faster my shins were moving on the end of the rotation. Now, imagine the force it took to stop that rotation and throw me in the complete opposite direction! How bad could it feel, and how much damage could it really do?

Yep, it would be like sitting in a chair and having Barry Bonds take a swing at your shins with an aluminum bat. I didn't feel the pain when I hit the bar, but I was pretty disoriented when I hit the mat, flipping in the opposite direction. I remember hitting the mat and pulling my knees to my chest to get a look at the damage.

This story isn't about being tough, but it is about having courage. I'll spare you the gore, but here's what the pursuit of my passion helped me to do. I was so passionate about taking my path as far as I could that I got my legs stitched up and made pads to cover the stitches.

You see, our team needed my score, and I needed the score to help me qualify for the end-of-year National Collegiate Athletic Association competitions. So, our team doctor molded fiberglass shin pads with foam protection on the inside (like a soccer shin-pad), and we cut out the padding where my stitches were, much like a doughnut hole.

The very next day, I had to be at practice to fix the mistake I made and build the confidence that I could do the dismount, not chicken out, and be able to compete. I can remember to this day, being on top of the bar, getting ready to do my dismount and seeing my hands trembling. I was scared shitless.

Now imagine me, the next day with stitches in my shins, putting my grips on. I knew how bad it was going to hurt just swinging through the bottom of bar with all my blood rushing into my stitches, then having to fly eleven feet in the air; flip twice, fully extended in a straight-body position, and land.

On top of that, in the front of my brain, what worried me more than the pain was the "What if? What if I got it wrong and hit the bar again with stitches already in my shins?" Oh crap.

So there I was, in practice, putting on my grips, thinking, "there is no way in hell I'm doing this." But my buddies were counting on my score, and I couldn't let them down. So, I chalked my hands up and got a lift up to the bar because I couldn't really jump the nine feet up to grab the bar. (My shins hurt!) I started to swing to see just how bad it was going to hurt, feeling the blood rush to my stitches, as the force of gravity and rotation pulled the blood down into my legs. Oh, I can't describe the pain of the blood rushing to the stitches in my shins, but I could clearly feel the stitches pulsating, like they had their own heart, as I hopped off to the ground. Yikes!!!!!!!!

So… I stop swinging without doing my dismount to catch my breath and let the pain subside. A few minutes went by, and then it was time for me to get after it and try the dismount, despite the pain and my worry.

My coach lifted me up to the bar, and I swung, so I was on top of the bar in a support position trying to muster the courage to do the dismount again. I'll never forget; I was on top of the bar, and even though I was gripping the bar tightly, I was looking at my hands, the ground nine feet below me, and I was shaking like a leaf.

Remember when I said I had a history of not letting go of the bar? So, I was up there, with my coach nine feet below and eight feet away from the bar as a spotter. I casted up to a handstand and swung around the bar once, twice, and just at the precise moment I needed to let go… I chickened out and held on. What a letdown! My fear got the best of me, and my shins were pulsing in pain again.

I was embarrassed, my teammates were shaking their heads, and my coach did his best to offer some encouragement. I went to the chalk box, and a couple of my teammates tried to build up my confidence. I had to get over that fear. I had to compete in three days. My team needed my score.

After a few minutes of psyching myself up, I walked over to the bar and got a lift up. I cleared my mind and pulled myself on top of the bar and tried to block out my worry. I told myself: "Just do it. You got this. Just relax, and rock it like you have a million times before."

I think all of the guys on my team could see how I was struggling to muster up the courage, and they started yelling words of encouragement. "C'mon! Do it, Jackson! You got this! Get after it!" but I really was scared shitless. Then with a deep breath, I casted off of the bar, and swung around as fast as I could once. My courage was growing. I was getting into the zone. Then I swung around twice. I was in my zone. At precisely the time I needed to get off the bar, I let go. At the exact right time, I flew eleven-plus feet in the air with a completely straight body and actually landed perfectly on my feet.

When I hit the ground, the gym erupted and everybody yelled for me. Holy cow, was I relieved. I actually couldn't believe I did it! To build my courage, I did it three more times that day, but then I stopped because of the pain.

Well, that's good and all, but the next day the pain was so bad, I couldn't train. Talk about a courage killer! Ugh! To make a long story short, at our competition the day after, I did one of the best sets of my life and nailed the routine.

After that injury, every time I trained and competed on high-bar, that injury was always in the back of my mind. Through developing the daily discipline of confronting and growing my courage, letting go of the bar got a little easier each time.

I've used that exact experience as a reminder to have the courage to keep pushing through my comfort zones and continually grow. This is my blueprint to get the most out of my life and overcome almost any obstacle that presents itself.

As a kid growing up, I had a deep love of adventure. My parents always encouraged me to be my best, to explore, and to have fun. As a young kid, I was having experiences in life most kids would dream about.

My biological father built airplanes that he could also fly. He took my brother and me on fishing adventures to Canada and introduced me to sports. I remember as a kid, my dad would hook the tale of his home-built airplane to the back of our van, put me in the cockpit, and do engine run-ups in the driveway.

An engine run-up is when you fire the motor and work the throttle through different levels. So, imagine me at no more than nine to twelve years old, with a leather flight cap on, sitting in the cockpit of the airplane smiling ear-to-ear. My dad would run me through a series of safety checks, walk to the front of the plane, and hand-start the propeller.

Imagine being a neighbor driving down the street and seeing an airplane connected to the back of a van, engine running, with a kid in the seat running the throttle. That must have been some sight!

As I got older, he would take my brother and me to the most northern part of Ontario, Canada to fish for walleye, northern pike, and lake trout. My dad did a really good job of teaching us outdoors skills. He spent a lot of time teaching us how to navigate water on the map, read the weather, make a safety shelter, and, most important, to get back to camp before sundown.

Before the days of GPS, you had to make sure you were in camp before dark because when the light begins to fade, it is virtually impossible to make out an entrance to a cove or bay you may be looking for. You can get lost super easily. Thankfully, he spent a good amount of time teaching us how hard it is to navigate on big bodies of water in times of bad weather and in bad light.

When we were able to demonstrate to him that we were able to successfully navigate, read the weather, and manage time, he began to let us fish on our own. At first he would restrict our fishing to days of only good weather and areas close to camp. Over time, our restrictions loosened, and we were able to go further in times of good weather and bad.

Looking back on it now, it's fun to remember some of the crazy things my brother and I did together. There are days that we would be caught on the water, just he and I, in crazy rainstorms miles from camp. I remember one storm that we were caught in that made the waves on the main body of water seem half the size of me. It may not be impressive by today's standards, but we were fishing in twelve-feet boats with five horsepower motors.

I can't remember how old I was, exactly, but I could not have been more than twelve years old, and I remember sitting in the back of the boat, with my brother driving, bailing water out of the back of the boat with a one-gallon milk carton with the bottom cut off. As we were making our way back to camp through the big waves, I was having the time of my life. At times, the water splash, generated by the bow of the boat hitting the waves, seemed to fill the boat faster than we could bail it out. Being in the big water in bad weather was always a little scary, but I was in love with the adventure.

The confidence my father instilled in me gave me a passion for adventure. It helped me realize that even though I might be trying something new, if I remember basic safety principles, I could be successful and have fun. I live by this principle to this day.

My mother and stepfather took our family to our lake house to swim and ski, exploring the city of Chicago and coordinating family events. We spent a lot of time together as a family. It's crazy to think of how normal I thought it was and how I believed every family must live this way.

He and my mother really pounded the value of hard work, honesty, and not giving up on your dreams in my head. They didn't simply talk about these values; they lived them. I remember them both working long hours and how, year after year, our life would always get more comfortable. They both sacrificed their time and money, so that my brother, sister, and I could play the sports we wanted and spend a lot of time at the lake having fun in the summers.

I always loved sports when I was a kid. We played outside sports all summer long. We would play pick-up baseball, football, basketball, and street hockey. Being one of the youngest, I was always trying to keep up with the older kids. I was blessed with good athleticism and coordination, but was short on size (no pun intended).

The one sport that stuck with me was gymnastics. For some reason, I loved the challenge. It was more than running a route, catching a ball, making a basket, or shooting a goal. To me it was so much more.

It satisfied my need for adventure because every day was a challenge to try something new and to go higher and farther than the day before. The adrenaline rush of walking the fine line of success and risking crash and burn injuries was too much to walk away from.

Living with my parents and playing gymnastics taught me that life is an adventure worth living when you pursue your passion. Your passion can bring out the best in you in ways you never have imagined. When I'm following my passions, I have more energy, happiness, confidence, love, patience, resilience, and focus than any other time of the day.

To this day, I feel more fulfilled from my infamous gymnastics injury and countless others just like it, than from any object I've bought or milestone I ticked off the list. Looking back, I often wondered why these moments fulfilled me so profoundly and made me feel so proud.

I now realize it's because of the feeling I get from knowing I overcame pain, doubt, and fear to grow and expand my abilities as person and a gymnast.

Fulfillment is about challenging ourselves, overcoming obstacles, and contributing to the betterment of others.

CHAPTER 2

CRY FOR HELP

> "The truth will set you free, but first it will piss you off."
> ~ Gloria Steinem

I started my insurance career in 2001, with the encouragement of a friend. It's not something that I ever thought I would do. I had just gotten out of a failed business partnership, a construction company formed on a handshake and dissolved with hard feelings on both sides. Looking for something to do and wanting to get out of the construction industry, I decided to reinvent myself. It turned to be one of the best decisions in my life.

I started by helping companies find affordable group health insurance and grew a successful practice. Two years into my career, I found myself still looking for growth opportunities, and I discovered the practice of advising companies, associations, and individuals on how to protect their retirement assets from the high cost of long-term health care, better known as Long Term Care Insurance (LTCI).

From 2003 to 2008, I built a very successful practice and gained a vast amount of experience and wisdom from working with clients aged 58 to 80. I had intuitively positioned my practice to be an independent brokerage firm, not beholden to any one particular carrier, and I had set up my compensation to be equally paid by all of the carriers I could represent. This was important to my clients because it communicated a core value of fairness—I could not be swayed by compensation to offer one carrier over another.

This corporate structure turned out to be one of the best decisions I made for years to come. I gained my clients' trust and respect because they knew that an independent adviser was authentically fairer when recommending appropriate tools to solve their problems. Many corporate advisers offer the same tool to solve different problems for different people. I'm not a big believer in the "one size fits all product" solution.

When the real estate correction of 2007 hit, followed by the stock market correction of 2008, most working Americans found that their dreams of security in retirement were completely shattered. Many Americans lost their homes AND almost half of their retirement savings. Financial devastation had hit America.

Talking with clients in 2007 and 2008, I got a real sense of their frustration, desperation, and fear. In the midst of the crisis, I was preaching to them about asset preservation, protecting retirement funds from another looming crisis, and the high cost of long-term health care for seniors and the disabled.

Early in 2009, I started getting the calls. "Matt, you did such a great job advising us on our retirement insurance, and we like your independent broker relationship. We trust you. Will you please help us with our investments? Since we lost a major part of our retirement savings, our broker won't return our calls. They've done nothing to protect us from the loss. Please help!"

As a guy who believes in fairness, these calls really pissed me off. These good people had hired trusted advisers to help them, and they weren't getting the help they were promised. I can't even count the amount of people I spoke to who had to go back to work in retirement, cut back their monthly budgets, and were emotionally devastated by their losses. Poor management had instantly undone a lifetime of saving. I'm not saying that good financial management would have prevented everyone from losing a large portion of their portfolio value, but I *am* saying, in my opinion, the losses could have been much less.

Listening to my clients' and friends' stories of the devastation they had experienced and how they had been affected planted a seed in me. I wanted to help, but I wasn't sure if I wanted to add another professional advisory service in an area that had so horribly failed its clientele.

CHAPTER 3
COMPANY VS. CLIENT FIRST

"If you change the way you look at things,
the things you look at change."
~ Wayne Dyer

2010 was a very important year for me and for my clients. I began researching the best relationship that I could bring to the table when helping them with their retirement finances. Like my insurance brokerage firm, it was important that I bring the best the industry has to offer in an independent relationship, one that puts the client's needs ahead of the investment provider's needs. My research revealed that this is known as a *fiduciary* relationship. Don't forget that term.

People inherently want the best, and they want to believe they are getting independent advice. But the dirty little industry secret I discovered through my research is that the vast majority of sales people offering financial investments don't play by those rules.

On February 1, 2010, an article in *The Wall Street Journal* reported that "In 2008, 17% of financial advisers were fee-only"[1]. This really bothered me because it meant that 83% of financial professionals were cleverly disguised sales people who, at the time, were receiving commission on the tools they recommended to clients AND they only had to abide by a *suitability* standard.

In 2009, *The Wall Street Journal* contributor Jason Zweig commented on the suitability standard, writing, "A key factor still is missing from FINRA's suitability requirements: cost. Let's say you tell your broker that you want to simplify your stock portfolio into an index fund. He then tells you that his firm manages an S&P-500 Index fund that is 'suitable' for you. He is under no obligation to tell you that the annual expenses that his firm charges on the fund are 10 times higher than an essentially identical fund from Vanguard. An adviser acting under fiduciary duty would have to disclose the conflict of interest and tell you that cheaper alternatives are available. If brokers had to take cost and conflicts of interest into account in order to honor a fiduciary duty to their clients, their firms might hesitate before producing the kind of garbage that has blighted the portfolios of investors over the years."[2]

Imagine my surprise at reading articles like this while researching the best way to help my future clients! What? You mean a lot of these people don't have to disclose a conflict of interest or explain that there are different alternatives with little or no cost? I had no idea what a fiduciary standard of care versus a suitable standard of care meant to the Main Street investor, but, for me, it solidified what had to be done.

In 2010, I was fortunate enough to meet a very special man, Mark Sorensen. He helped me fit all of the pieces of the puzzle together. Mr. Sorensen laid it all out on the table for me, and I'm going to relay his wisdom to you.

I heard Mark speak at a conference about the benefits of being an independent fee-based fiduciary adviser and how it was the best relationship to bring to the table for the client. Mark spoke passionately and confidently about how much of the retirement investment sales system was rigged against the Main Street investor and how the suitability standard harmed the client.

He challenged us to think of it in these terms. There is an absolute war going on for an investor's money. The war is between companies that offer securities based tools (i.e. wirehouse, brokerage firms, and banks) and companies that offer safe products (i.e. insurance companies). If you see a person for advice who only holds a securities license, they will only tell you about the virtues of securities-based products. If you see a person for advice who only holds an insurance license, they will only tell you of the virtues of insurance-based products. Neither has any incentive to tell you about the benefits of the other's solutions for two reasons.

#1 If you only hold a securities license, you can only talk about what? Securities! And if you only hold an insurance license you can only talk about what? Insurance! Do you see the problem here?

#2 If a salesperson's compensation is based upon the securities products they sell, why would they ever tell you, the client, about the benefits of insurance products, when they make no money? If a salesperson's compensation is based on the sale of insurance products, why would they ever tell the client about the benefits of securities products, when they make no money?

It's like going into a Ford dealership and telling them everything you want in a new sedan. Do you think you are ever going to hear their salesperson say Chevrolet is a much better fit for you? Heck no! It's no different in the retirement investing/planning business!

Have you ever wondered how what you own in your retirement portfolio can largely be influenced by how the person who is giving you the advice is licensed? Later, I'm going to reveal why you are encouraged to have 100% of your money invested in the stock market and why you may not want to have all of your retirement savings invested in the stock market.

THE WAR OVER YOUR MONEY

CHAPTER 4
ESSENTIALS OF PLANNING

"There's a way to do it better. Find it."
~ Thomas Edison

Many of you may have just learned for the first time that there can be biases and conflicts of interest that affect the type of retirement investment advice you receive. It probably seems normal to have 100% of your money invested in the stock market. After all, that is what you've been told and, later in this book, I'll reveal why and how that notion is reinforced.

Let me share a story with you regarding about when you retire affects how you retire. Meet Jack and Jill Mainstreet. Like many Americans, Jack and Jill worked hard all of their adult lives to save for their dream retirement. They didn't eat out as much as they would have liked and delayed vacations and newer cars in order to fund their retirement accounts as much possible.

Jack and Jill's retirement date was December of 2006. They thought they were doing everything right. They had a balanced portfolio of stock, bonds and mutual funds invested 100 percent in the stock market. They had figured in retirement they could live off of the interest their principle was producing in retirement. Their retirement account balance reached $800,000. If they could withdraw five percent annually from their portfolios, they would have

$40,000 of annual income, enough income in retirement to live comfortably when added to their social security benefits.

December 2006 comes, and they have a nice party. They celebrate enduring years of working, saving and sacrificing. Job well done! They enjoyed a few months of worry-free retirement, but they were noticing the effects of an over-inflated housing market in the economy. There wasn't much to worry about because this is America, and bad times don't last long.

But the slide kept coming. Over the years, the home Jack and Jill had lived in for twenty-plus years had increased in value nicely… on paper. They had planned on downsizing in retirement and enjoying the appreciation in the form of cash from the sale of their home in retirement. But the slide kept coming! According to the Case-Shiller home price index, property values hit their lowest low on December 30, 2008. Jack and Jill saw their paper appreciation evaporate in 24 months. Selling for the profit they had hoped, and planned on, wouldn't be happening.

To add insult to injury, the American stock market experienced it's largest sell-off in modern history. Like many Americans, Jack and Jill saw a 42 percent drop in value in their retirement account, while in retirement! The reality of creating the monthly retirement income they needed to live on by withdrawing 5 percent from their portfolio was shattered.

Their portfolio value had vanished by 42 percent. It was down to $464,000. Jack and Jill did some recalculating. In order to create the same income from their investments in retirement, Jack and Jill now calculated they would need to withdraw 8.8% from their portfolios, but now that interest rates and returns were essentially zero they would have to chip away at their principle savings… significantly.

Jack and Jill decide to go back to work to make up the shortfall, but that was a problem. Who was going to hire a retiree in the middle of a recession? Retirees are expensive, pricier than millennials. Worry sets in. Are Jack and

Jill going to be able to live the retirement they dreamed of? Are they going to be able to pursue their passions they delayed because of work and saving? Do you know a Jack and Jill? Chances are you do. We all do.

If Jack and Jill had not invested 100 percent of their retirement in the stock market, this might have been prevented. Had Jack and Jill structured their retirement slightly differently, they may have been able to save themselves from sleepless nights, frustration, and heartache.

I'm going to let you in on a nice secret. Retirement is about asset preservation with some accumulation rather than just accumulation. Instead of relying on non-protected returns, a secure income and asset security could have given Jack and Jill the confidence to chase their passions in retirement.

Having helped many pre-retirees and retirees, I believe that the heavy lifting of saving and accumulating should be mostly completed during working years. When the working years are over you should have enough to live comfortably on. There should be no need to take on the risk of being 100 percent invested in something you cannot and do not have any control over. As we just were reminded in the story above. It can be a recipe for disaster.

You may be thinking, what was I supposed to do? Let's talk about asset preservation strategies versus asset accumulation strategies. It's quite simple, but important for you to understand. You can apply this principle effectively, but it may take a little reshaping of the construct you've been forced to believe.

I define asset preservation strategies as money that generally has low to moderate returns, but cannot be lost by a stock market sell-off. On the flip side, I define asset accumulation strategies as money that has highly variable returns and the risk of loss (sometimes significant loss).

Individuals and institutions are attracted to asset accumulation strategies, because they offer the opportunity for gains greater than inflation and we are told professional money managers are good at mitigating the risk of loss. However, we know that even the best money managers have a hard time predicting stock market sell-offs, proven in recent memory by the losses of 1987, 2000-2001, and 2007-2008.

Individuals and institutions are attracted to asset preservation strategies, because they offer slow consistent growth and peace of mind. The thought of losing a penny can keep some people awake at night. In this type of person's mind, a consistent two to five percent return, over time, may produce better returns over a long period of time, asset accumulation strategies. Plus, there is no worry if there is a major sell-off or decline in stock market values.

So, in a nutshell, people trade peace of mind for low returns, or they trade the thrill of success/ agony of defeat for the greater opportunity of higher returns. Which one are you? Are you the person who likes to gamble everything, even your profits, in Las Vegas? Or, do you prefer to limit the money you risk when you gamble, putting a portion of what you win away as you keep playing. Perhaps, you prefer not to gamble at all?

I'm quite sure most people are a little of both. I can't recall that I've ever met anyone in my life who would gamble their entire life savings recklessly. I've also never met someone who's never played a one-dollar card game with family and friends.

The point is, it's wise to have some money to use for higher returns, but a larger portion of money to squirrel away for the future, knowing it will always be there. It's my advice to use the same strategy in your retirement portfolio.

So what are the asset preservation strategies and asset accumulation strategies available to you? It's really quite simple. You probably know 90 percent of what I'm going to share with you, because it's what we've been led to believe for the last fifty years. Keep reading! The other 10 percent may significantly change the way you think about saving and investing in retirement.

Asset Accumulation Strategies

Generally speaking, asset accumulation strategies include stocks, bonds, mutual funds, variable annuities and real estate investment trusts (REITS). These solutions do not provide guarantees against loss, but they do provide the opportunity for returns better than inflation. They are typically provided by stockbrokers, wire-houses, financial advisers and the big banks I mentioned earlier.

Picking individual stocks can be an intimidating for individuals who are not familiar with profit and loss statements, earning reports, etc. I do believe it is possible to pick one stock, hold it for a long time and win. The problem is if you are not doing this on your own, your stockbroker will discourage this because there is not money in it for them or their company. They get paid on the transactions of you buying and selling stocks inside your portfolio.

Here's a great example to remember. If I'm a commissions-based stockbroker I'm looking for someone to sell my recommendations to, so I can make a living. The cycle typically goes like this. I call a client and say, "Hey Jack, according to our research, Google is going to be a big winner soon. Let's buy." Jack trusts me, and he agrees to buy Google. Four months later I call Jack and say, "Hey Jack, Google did great the last four months, but our research is showing that Apple is going to be a bigger winner. Let's buy." Jack trusts me and he sells Google and buys Apple.

As a stockbroker, what did I just do? I made three commissions in four months. I had a client buy Google, then sell Google, then buy Apple. No problem, as long as each transaction results in a gain to you, as the client. We all know too well that "timing the market" can be a recipe for disaster, and many people have won and lost "timing the market". Buying a stock and sticking to it is easy to do, but as you see not so easy to do.

Why do I include bonds in this category? Bonds do hold interest rate risk. Meaning, bond returns are tied to interest rates. As interest rates decrease, bond returns increase. This is why bonds had such a great run of success from the mid-1980s. Interest rates had done nothing but decrease the last three decades.

On the flip side, as interest rates increase, bond returns decrease. So where are interest rates now? Essentially zero. Where do we all know interest rates are heading in the future? Up! So you see, bonds do hold risk as well. Be careful.

Variable annuities are nothing more than mutual funds and are sold for their ability to create guaranteed income. In my analysis, these solutions typically have expense charges two to five times higher than a normal IRA and provide no guarantees for your cash against loss. Some do provide guaranteed lifetime income, but they are often tied to the performance inside the plan.

In years of great returns these can be good plans. Buyer beware, you can still lose your shorts if there is a decline in market value, like in the recent past.

Mutual funds and Real Estate Investment Trusts (REITs) are sold to the public with the premise that diversification mitigates risk. I agree they can mitigate risk by diversifying the holdings inside those solutions, but we all know too well, there are no guarantees against loss.

There are two reasons why mainstream investment management companies (stockbrokers and big banks) steer their clients' assets into these strategies. First, they obviously make really nice commissions when you buy individual stocks, Class A, Class B, Class C mutual funds, and non-publically traded REITS. Have you ever wondered why you hold Class-A mutual funds in your portfolio? You should.

Second, these companies and individuals do not have the proper licensing to even talk about the asset preservation strategies I'm going to share with you next. This never made sense to me, because if they advise people on how best to save for retirement, why wouldn't they want to bring all of the necessary tools to the table to ensure the best success for the client?

Well, I refer you back to the first reason. These institutions would likely make more money over a long period of time by keeping investors 100 percent invested in the stock market, no matter the outcome of your performance. They are making money based upon the sale of securities not the performance of the securities. This is why, in my opinion, they have no incentive to tell you the value of transitioning a large portion of your retirement to asset preservation strategies near or in retirement.

So to recap, these institutions and individuals hide asset preservation strategies from the public, even demonize them, because they are, most likely, not licensed to talk about them. Plus, even if they were, they would make less money, over time, if their clients used asset preservation strategies rather than being 100 percent invested in the stock market their entire lives.

Asset Preservation Strategies

Generally speaking, asset preservation strategies include bank CDs, treasuries, some bonds, cash, fixed annuities, fixed index annuities (FIA's) and cash-value life insurance. They are typically provided by bank representatives and licensed insurance advisers. Easy enough, right? Wrong. Not all asset preservation strategies are created equally.

Many have interest rate risk. Interest rate risk is the erosion of the value of your money because the return of the plan is less than how inflation is growing (this is called negative *arbitrage*).

If a bank CD, money market account, fixed annuity, municipal bond, or treasury bill are not growing at a greater rate than the cost of inflation, the value of your money will become less over time. Simple math: If the safe money solution return is 1.2%, but inflation is 3%, your return is -1.8% per year.

Although that is better than a five to ten percent loss with a stock market sell-off, in my mind it's not really a asset preservation strategy, especially if the interest rate is fixed and inflation is a moving target.

Some fixed index annuities do a better job of hedging against interest rate risk than others. The strategies I prefer have returns tied to the performance of a professionally managed index (fancy word for mutual fund) and have no direct downside market risk.

Think of them in these terms. They are essentially professionally managed mutual funds, without the direct downside market risk if the stock market has a sell-off or declines in value. In the last five years, insurance companies have been partnering with professionally managed indexes to provide clients with the opportunity to outpace inflation without opening up to the direct downside of market loss inherent in the stock market.

If you could go to Las Vegas and play a game where every time you won, the house simply kept 1% to 1.5% of your winnings, but every time you lost, they simply kept your original bet on the table and didn't take your bet away? Would you play? Heck yes! I would play that game all day. That's the simplified version of how the fixed indexed annuities, I like, work.

Some cash value life insurance solutions work much the same way. Your cash deposit can participate in the growth of an index AND provide a life insurance death benefit to your heirs. I like these plans in terms of their ability to multiply your money in retirement.

Properly designed plans allow for cash accumulation, benefits for long-term health care needs, and a tax-free death benefit to heirs. Multiplying your money in retirement can be a very powerful tool for the right people.

Many people reading about the benefits I just described, have never heard about the benefits of these plans. You may be wondering if they are not too good to be true. I hear it all the time. The truth is that fixed index annuities and cash-value life insurance work very well and are very effective in protecting and multiplying the value of retirement plans in life and death.

Hopefully, you now you realize that you may have not heard about the benefits of these plans because of the bias and conflict of interest that goes on in the investing world. It's my hope that I have opened your mind to more options available to you that can increase your chances of protecting your profits and building your confidence that your retirement will not be wiped away in another stock market sell-off.

In this chapter, we learned how many good investors lost a major portion of their retirement savings to external forces they have no control over (the stock market). In our story, we saw how being 100 percent invested in asset accumulation strategies is a recipe for disaster in retirement and offers little to no guarantees when it comes to providing lifetime income in retirement.

Conversely, we explored the benefits of transitioning from 100 percent asset accumulation strategies to asset preservation strategies when near and/or in retirement. By transitioning to more asset preservation strategies, investors can secure a large portion of the retirement savings from stock market losses and take more control over their life savings, and they don't need to sacrifice good returns to get safety.

We explored the definition and examples of asset preservation strategies and asset accumulation strategies and you should now understand why investors are kept in the dark about the benefits of securing their hard-earned retirement savings from being 100 percent invested in something they have no control over (the stock market).

Finally, I shared with you how I recommend my private clients structure their retirement savings for their benefit. I believe that when retirement plans are structured this way, it gives investors an understanding of the purpose of their money and what their money is accomplishing for them.

Thinking of your money in these terms can help solidify the amounts of assets you allocate for each specific purpose. It will also help you decide what types of solutions will help you best accomplish these goals and how much money you need to have allocated in "Asset Accumulation Strategies" and "Asset Preservation Strategies" to ensure a safe and secure retirement. The ultimate goal, for me, is to give my clients and you the ability to follow their passions in retirement with confidence, free of financial uncertainty and anxiety.

I know from experience that the only way people feel they have permission to create a fulfilling retirement, full of personal growth and new challenges, is by creating safety and security in the retirement plan.

In my experience, having enough immediate money available, putting income-producing money to proper use, and being able to multiply legacy money in retirement mentally gives retirees' permission to pursue their real passions.

This is my hope for you too!

BREAK THIS CONSTRUCT

> "Wealth is the ability to fully experience life."
> ~ Henry David Thoreau

The old style of asset accumulation is not right during retirement!

One of the greatest privileges I've experienced in my career is encouraging people to go out there and shape new habits and inspiring them to really go for it. I'm going to share with you some of the things I have done to help people shape new habits.

Many people have come to me feeling helpless, and pessimistic, about what the future holds for them. Their retirement plans are not structured correctly, so they feel a lot of discontent and anxiety around the fact that they may outlive their money in retirement.

When retirement plans are not structured correctly, focusing more on asset accumulation than asset preservation, it creates anxiety because people are waiting for the next crash. They can almost feel that the floor is about to drop out. They are waiting for the good times to end.

I've been able to show people a better way of structuring their retirement, one that establishes guarantees and safety while still getting good returns. It has given people the permission to feel that their lives are going to be OK. without blowing up their retirement plan, it gives people a chance to live their retirement to its fullest.

It's amazing how easily people can get stuck in their daily routine when they don't know, definitively, that they will not outlive their money in retirement. When I've been able to give my clients a lot more certainty that their money is going to last, even through the bad times, it's fun to watch them shake off their anxiety, take a deep breath of fresh air, and really live life the way that they want to.

It's in you too! You can do anything you want in retirement, but you need to make sure that your retirement plan is structured correctly. Your money can outlast you in retirement. Give yourself the luxury of safety. Give yourself the luxury of guaranteed income. Give yourself the luxury of confidence in retirement.

Unfortunately, most people in my business will not do the right thing when it comes to sharing the proper strategies and tools that give pre-retirees and retirees the ability to shape new habits. So, drum up the courage to go find the people I described on pages 21 -22 who will do the right thing for *you*. Find the people who don't just do the right thing for their corporate and personal pocketbook.

Find the courage and determination to find the person who will help *you* best. This is the person who understands the importance of shifting from asset accumulation to more asset preservation, so you can decrease the anxiety in your life and follow your passions with less anxiety and more confidence your money will last your lifetime.

You *can* find those people. You now have the knowledge of what to look for in trustworthy and knowledgeable advisers to explore what's best for you. At the end of the day, if you take the time to interview five planners, and four don't fit the criteria I outline in the book, it was time well spent increasing your chances of having the confident retirement you've intuitively wanted but not been able to find.

This is so important for your confidence. I've interviewed many pre-retirees and retirees about what worries them most in retirement. The most common response I've received is not if they have enough money to retire. In fact, the biggest and most common source of anxiety pre-retirees and retirees have is how they will be affected if there is another market sell-off or crash. I'm sure that this concern contributes to the fact that there is, at the time of publication, an estimated $3 trillion of investable money sitting on the sidelines. This is money either sitting in a money market, checking or savings account, a bank CD; or stuffed under a mattress.

We need to break the old method of structuring retirement plans. Incorrectly structured plans cause uncertainty. People fear that retirement savings may be wiped out by the next bad tweet, missed earnings report, election, terrorist attack, or tax policy. These fears are causing people to miss out on a blissful retirement.

When I've asked those same exact people what would help to ease their fears, the response I most commonly receive is "I want to know my retirement income and savings will last through another correction or crash. I want to know I won't have to go back to work. I want to know I'm not going to lose my money".

To get a better understanding of how these same people may best go about doing that, my next question is, "Do you have any idea how to do that?"

I typically get two answers to this question.

1. "I have a bunch of money sitting in a money market, checking, or savings account." OR... "It's in my safe at home, and although I know it's safe and I can't lose it to things not in my control, I do understand that the value of my money is being eroded by inflation

and/or the opportunity loss of not being invested in anything that offers better returns than what I'm getting, typically 1 percent or less. Those problems are giving me anxiety, similar to what I would feel if I were invested in the stock market. I'm torn because I'm damned if I do, damned if I don't. But, I do know that not losing a major portion of my retirement savings is the lesser of two evils, as opposed to getting very little in return. I want better than 1 percent returns, but I don't want to sacrifice safety."

2. "I have no idea and that's why I'm here. I don't know of any other opportunities other than what is being pushed on me by my stockbroker, and my intuition is telling me there is something more out there."

People fear that retirement savings may be wiped out by the next bad tweet, missed earnings report, election, terrorist attack, or tax policy. These fears are *causing people to miss out on a blissful retirement.*

Those 2 typical habitual answers also need to be broken.

This old style of investing is now habitually engrained year after year into people approaching and entering retirement. If you want safety and security, you have to sacrifice good returns (3 percent to 9 percent would fit my definition of good returns), and you really have no way to create guaranteed income in the asset accumulation style of retirement structuring being pushed on the public.

The standard structure of building retirement plans offers little safety, security, or guaranteed income. The cycle must be broken to give individuals what they truly deserve in retirement. People deserve safety, security, guaranteed income, liquidity for emergency, and tax-efficient legacy gifting. The structure that denies them this is what needs to be broken.

These old habits are powerful, and the way they are engrained and perpetuated on the public are powerful. Many of you, for the first time, are understanding that it is possible to break the powerful habit of improperly structured retirement plans for pre-retirees and retirees. Many of you, for the first time, now know that there are ways to overcome the insecurities stirring in your gut through using tools and strategies that are being kept from you.

Many of you, for the first time, are realizing that the reason this style of structuring retirement plans has been kept from you or demonized to you by stockbrokers and big banks is because they are either not licensed to offer them, or they would make less money if you used them in your retirement plan. If you think about it, if a brokerage firm or big bank made less money educating their clients about these strategies, they would have no incentive to spend the money licensing or training their people about the advantages of structuring retirement the way we have been talking about. Ugh!

I've seen this have a direct cause and effect on the mental health of retirees. The insecure structure of retirement plans and the stock market crashes we've had to live through have caused the public to be very mistrusting of the institutions and individuals giving investment and retirement advice. Rightly so! However, you now have the tools to break these powerful bad past habits.

By having the knowledge of how to structure retirement plans with safety and guaranteed income, you can give yourself the confidence to go live your life passions, knowing your retirement income will last and grow throughout the economic ups and downs through your retirement. By decreasing your stress and anxiety, in anticipation of the next market crash, you free up your energy and intuition to pursue the life you want to live.

Imagine not having the gut-wrenching feeling of worrying about what is happening to your retirement account with the next market swing. Imagine feeling more confident in the value of your assets even in the face of events you can't control, like the latest terror attack or impending Presidential election. Imagine knowing you can live a life true to yourself, without worrying about what is happening in the news tomorrow and how it's going to affect your income in retirement. Imagine not letting life pass you by just because you're holding on to your money tightly in anticipation of the next market correction.

If you were able to let all of that anxiety go, would you live life a little differently? Would you quit delaying buying your dream house or car? Would you quit delaying helping people, charities, of following your passions? Would you have the confidence to loosen your purse strings to live more comfortably? Would you feel more optimistic that you can grow in different areas of your life? Would you feel that if your dream pursuit costs you money, it's OK, because you'd rather it be spent growing your passions then lost in a market sell-off?

In my experience, when I've been able to help people break these old habits, the answer is "YES"! In fact, these people say they are more optimistic about their retirement. Anxiety is not looming in their heart. Anticipating bad news leading to a major loss of their retirement accounts doesn't keep them up at night, and they can focus more on happiness then thinking "what if I lose it all"?

Your Personal Strategy Session

Have you ever put off doing something because you were uncertain how it would affect your finances?

What would you do, right now, if you had more confidence in your finances?

Take out a note pad and list the top three things.

CHAPTER 5
THE DISCONNECTED INVESTOR

> "We choose our joys and sorrows
> long before we experience them."
> ~ Khalil Gibran

The greatest gift I've received from the thousands of personal interviews I've completed over the years is the ability to observe people in retirement and the type of life they are living. It's given me the ability to look at my life in retirement and to find new ways to shape my experience.

By digging into my clients' lives, I've observed the poor decisions people have made and the hardships they have endured in their working lives to put them into a place of insecurity and worry in retirement. There have also been many great examples and role models of people who have made good decisions during working years to put their families in very solid, secure, and fulfilling retirements.

Making good decisions regarding money is an important part of that equation, but decisions about family, children, health, wellness, charity, work, personal growth and hobbies are a huge part of the equation as well.

THE DISCONNECTED INVESTOR

One of the saddest stories I continue to hear repeatedly is the story of the Disconnected Investor.

Let's call our disconnected investor Bruce. He's the fella we all know. Bruce, at age 60, works a good nine-to-five job, and he is a dedicated employee who diligently contributes to his corporate 401(k) plan and a personal individual retirement account (IRA) . Bruce is like most people who rely on a 401(k) plan provider to give him the best advice on the available investment choices. He trusts his employer has picked a trustworthy 401(k) administrator that offers the best investment choices at the lowest cost.

Bruce meets with a 401(k) plan representative once per year for twenty minutes to review his performance for the past year and think about changing any strategies used in the previous year. Bruce is intimidated by investment language and concepts, and he has never really taken the time to understand the basics of how investments work. After all, they are written in a language no one seems to understand.

Consequently, he does not know how to dissect a performance report. He also has no idea what questions to ask in order to increase his chances for the best growth potential in the coming year. So, not wanting to seem foolish at his meeting with the 401(k) plan adviser, Bruce nods his head through the meetings and changes nothing year to year.

The 401(k) plan representatives love Bruce because he puts up no resistance to their recommendations, and they get to move on to the next employee quickly. Bruce doesn't mind because he feels like he can't really control what happens with his investments, so why should he bother spending the time to really learn his options?

2006 is a great year for Bruce. At his annual performance review, he learns his returns are acceptable, and he decides not to make any changes to his portfolio. Bruce feels good about the advice he receives because he is using professionally managed mutual funds comprised of stocks. He's feeling bullet-proof and content about the way things are heading and how his retirement accounts are performing.

> The next two years are a total different story for Bruce. In 2007, the real estate bubble crash hits. Bruce seems paralyzed; he feels unable to move any of his investments at his next annual review. The investments have performed well in the past, and his 401(k) plan representatives are not anticipating huge changes in the stock market. He, again, makes no choices.

In 2008, Bruce loses 37.7 percent of his total retirement plan savings. It's a devastating loss, and the only advice Bruce's 401(k) plan adviser offer is to continue to hold his investments and hope everything comes back. Bruce was burned with the tech bubble crash in 2000-2001. He's fed up, frustrated, and worried about investing in a system he does not understand. Can you relate?

Bruce starts talking to his friends and asking what they are doing in the face of financial destruction. Bruce's friends tell him to either put his money in a cash account or to buy bond funds. Unsure of what to do, Bruce decides to put his 401(k) assets into a mutual fund comprised of "safe" bonds and moves the money in his IRA into cash.

He feels that this is the best thing to do because he's been told it's very hard to lose with bonds, and everyone he knows got hurt just as badly as he did, and they are doing the same thing. Bruce is so fed-up and frustrated with the performance of his investments that he decides to check out of worrying about his performance and stops communicating with his 401(k) and IRA representatives. After all, what good has it gotten him? He feels he can't trust their advice.

The Dow Jones Industrial Average (DJIA) hits the lowest low on March 9, 2009. The index is at 6594.94 points and is down from the December 31, 2008 close of 8776.39. Bruce is feeling pretty good about his choices to move his money to cash and bonds.

As if the pain of losing 37.7% of his retirement wasn't bad enough, it gets worse. Bruce loses the opportunity to recover his losses. From March 9, 2009 to January 4, 2010, the market climbs to 10,583 points, but Bruce is invested in bonds and rather than seeing his accounts increase significantly, he sees a pathetic 2% growth. Still worried about the losses of 2007 and 2008, Bruce avoids his annual review and doesn't change a thing with his investment accounts.

The DJIA grows from 10,583 points on January 4, 2010 to 11,722 points on January 5, 2011. Bruce's performance is lagging far behind how the DJIA is performing, but Bruce can't stomach the idea of losing again. He follows his friends' advice of being conservative and not buying into a market at new all-time highs. He listens to his self-proclaimed expert friends and believes the market is overpriced.

Bruce knows there is an election in 2012 and feels very uncertain about what the economy might do. There is an impending "fiscal cliff" in the government, and tax policy could change, among other factors. Bruce chooses to stay safe in 2012 and makes no changes. The DJIA continues to climb and closes on December 30, 2012 at 12,217.56 points.

Disgusted with his bond portfolio's low performance and a lack of trust in his 401(k) plan advisers, Bruce continues to be disconnected from his investments and chooses to make no changes in 2013.

The election process is over. Bruce is feeling better about the uncertainty elections bring. He's considering making changes in 2014 to his accounts. Bruce just can't get his head around what his next step should be. Even though the DJIA has doubled in value since March 9, 2009, he just can't figure out when the best time would be to make a change. It seems as if every gain in the last 3.5 years has been met with downward adjustments, which causes fear of another slide.

Despite various scenarios that cause temporary decreases in value, the market continues to grow. The naysayers on television are still talking about the next crash, and Bruce can still remember the gut-wrenching feeling of losing almost 40 percent of his hard-earned cash. Even worse, he's further behind because he's lost out on the recent growth and is more frustrated than ever.

2013 starts off fast, and the DJIA grows exponentially until July. From July to December, the market is relatively flat. It has three sell-offs in that time, which cause concerns, but it does finish the year up quite a bit. On January 3, 2014, the DJIA closes at 16,469 points. Bruce is feeling the pressure of getting back in the market, but the late year sell-offs have him worried. Again, Bruce leaves his investments as is.

From January 3, 2014 to December 31, 2014 the DJIA grows to 17,823 points. It's time for Bruce's annual 401(k) plan review. Frustrated by the past five years, Bruce makes an appointment with the 401(k) plan representatives. After reviewing his lack of performance and talking with the representatives, Bruce agrees to make some changes to investment holdings.

Bruce invests in mutual funds comprised of stocks and target date funds. The DJIA climbs to 18,232 points on May 22, 2015. Bruce is feeling great about his choice to sell his bond holding and enjoy faster growth. Then the unthinkable happens. From May 22, 2015 to December 31, 2015, the DJIA starts a big backslide, and the DJIA closes at 16,346 points on January 8, 2016, down almost 10%. The small gains he made the last six years have been completely wiped out, and he's lost even more. Feeling like he has nothing to lose, Bruce skips his 2016 annual meeting with his 401(k) representatives and completely disconnects from his retirement savings accounts. Thankfully, since January 8, 2016, the DJIA has made a remarkable rally and continues to grow to new all-time highs.

	Bruce	DJIA
01/01/07 – 01/01/09	- 37.7%	- 42%
01/01/09 – 01/01/10	+ 2%	+ 21%
01/01/10 – 01/04/11	+ 2%	+ 11%
01/05/11 – 01/01/13	+ 4%	+ 7%
01/02/13 – 01/04/14	+ 2%	+ 36%
01/05/14 – 01/01/15	+ 2%	+ 9.5%
01/02/15 – 01/08/16	- 11.5%	- 11.5%
Total hypothetical change in value	- 37.2%	+ 31%
From 01/01/07 – 01/01/15		

* DJIA annual gains and losses are approximate #'s rounded.

Hopefully, you don't have a knot in your stomach reading about Bruce's chain of circumstances and decisions. Painfully, I continue to hear these about stories of how people have become disconnected to their finances. These types of stories inspire me to encourage change and to provide a framework for how you can begin to reshape your thinking around structuring your retirement savings.

Knowing we cannot change the past, I like to encourage people to change and improve for the future. First, work with a trusted adviser who understands the value of transparency, access to education, fiduciary-based independent advice and how to categorize your finances into the three categories I talk about later in chapter 23.

It's never too late to educate yourself on how to read a Morningstar report on investment choices. Morningstar is an independent third party organization. They provide all of the essential data a person needs to understand about securities registered options. The reports may look intimidating, but once you know the four to six information points you need to focus on you can make well-informed decisions about the investments you are considering.

Your Personal Strategy Session

One major reason people feel disconnected from their finances stems from how performance reports are structured. Do you like getting your quarterly fifteen-page investment report? Do you even understand how to read them? Most of people coming into my office hate those reports and have no idea how to read them. You are not alone.

Those reports can make very intelligent people feel foolish for not understanding them. Most reports I've reviewed in my office do a very poor job of communicating the bottom line. It's all about performance.

Here's how I recommend you solve the problem. Find a firm that will send you a simple one-page weekly report. It simply communicates where the investment value was at the beginning of the week and where it finished at the end of the week. I believe people feel connected when they see weekly investment performance in good times and bad. From my experience, transparency and access to information empowers people to get reconnected with their investments. In can be the same for you!

We all know and expect investments will go up and down. That's fine. It's my experience that people love to see the increases in weekly values, but appreciate the courage of communication when the account experiences a loss during the week. People I work with understand market fluctuations happen week to week and they really just want to know what it means to them in dollars and cents.

CHAPTER 6
THE CONNECTED INVESTOR

"Without knowledge action is useless
and knowledge without action is futile."
~ Abu Bakr

I wrote earlier that one great benefit of doing the work I do is witnessing the consequences of bad choices and negative events in people's retirement plans and learning how to troubleshoot and avoid them. I've also had the good fortune of seeing how positive choices and events people have experienced can put them in a good position for retirement.

I'd like to share the story of the connected investor with you. It's a story that starts out much like our friend Bruce's did. She's our neighbor. We'll call her Amy. Amy is a 64-year-old, recently retired divorcée of 10 years.

As Amy neared retirement at the beginning of 2006, she reviewed her investment statements and knew that all of her choices to live frugally and have a disciplined savings plan had paid off. Amy had amassed $750,000 in her 401(k).

The company Amy worked for does not offer a retirement pension. She would have to ensure her savings would last throughout her retirement. At age 65, Amy was eligible to collect her social security pension from the government.

Her annual social security income would be a little more that $28,000 annually. She wanted to have a target income of $50,000, beginning in 2006, for the rest of her retirement years.

That may not seem like much, but Amy had little to no expenses, and she could live comfortably on that income. She knew she had to withdraw $22,000 from her retirement account annually to meet her goal. But, she wondered, what would be the best way to go about doing that?

In preparation for retirement, Amy had done her homework. She spoke with friends, and, just by chance, she found an independent retirement planning specialist, recommended highly by a friend. She was hesitant to meet with this adviser, but after some encouragement from her friend, she decided she had nothing to lose and agreed to a free courtesy visit just to see what was out there.

At the meeting, the adviser advised her on the importance of independent status and shared the company's ability to offer insurance strategies as well as securities strategies. He also laid out the benefits of working with a retirement planning specialty firm. The adviser went on to explain the firm's corporate philosophy of compiling the best of the insurance and securities world to create plans that work synergistically.

Over the course of a few more months and visits, Amy realized that being 100 percent invested in the stock market was risky, and she needed to make her $750,000 last the rest of her life.

One the advice of her newly hired adviser, at the time of retirement (early 2006), Amy decided to move her 401(k) savings to her own IRA held at a custodial bank. Once the funds were electronically transferred to the new account, Amy and her adviser got to work.

Her adviser built a plan to reposition 70 percent of her $750,000 into an fixed indexed annuity that would grow her income-producing money by a guaranteed 7 percent per year. Their plan was to allow this $525,000 grow for five years and then begin her guaranteed income payment at age 70. Amy understood that by depositing money into this plan, the income-producing provision in the plan would grow by the guaranteed 7 percent, and if the stock market roared and earned more, well, then that would be the way it went. But, she also understood that if there were a crash similar to the bursting of the technology bubble in 2001 to 2002, she would not suffer much because she had sheltered a large portion of her savings.

The adviser explained that if she waited to turn on the guaranteed income provision of her plan at age 70, the insurance company would pay her 5 percent of her account value for life. That's right! For life! This means that the $525,000 growing by 7 percent for five years would have grown to $787,949 at the beginning of 2011 and would pay her approximately $39,397.45 for the rest of her life.

She felt really comfortable with this strategy because her needs for income would be met in five short years. Her social security payment, without an annual increase factored in, was $28,000, and her guaranteed income plan would add an additional $39,397.45, creating an income of $67,397.45 annually. This was more than enough to meet her income goal of $50,000 annually, and she'd even have extra funds to play with each year.

She and her adviser agreed to put the other 30 percent ($225,000) of her money to work in an account of managed mutual funds in the stock market. So let's see how her life over the next five years hypothetically played out.

On January 1, 2006, her beginning investment balance was $225,000. She withdrew $22,000 and put it into a savings account at the beginning of the year to add to her monthly social security check in order to create her $50,000 annual income.

In 2006, her performance lagged the average return of the Dow Jones

Industrial Average (DJIA), and her account grows by 15 percent. At the beginning of 2007, Amy had 233,450.00.

In January of 2007, Amy withdrew $22,000 and dropped it into her savings account. Her investment account earned 5 percent, still lagging the performance of the DJIA. At the end of 2007, Amy had $222,022 in her investment account.

In January of 2008, Amy withdrew $22,000, and deposited her money into her savings account, and then the bottom dropped out of the stock market. She lost 42 percent of her account value. At the end of December her account value had been significantly diminished to $136,015. That's a big hit!

Amy knew that if she could make that $136,000 last two more years, she would be home free because she could still turn on her guaranteed income-producing plan and have plenty of money. She was concerned, though, and met with her adviser.

The adviser reviews the fact that her income-producing account value had grown from $525,000 to $643,147.58, despite the market sell-off. She was so relieved! Her adviser recommended that she adjust her investments and keep the faith that she would be O.K. in retirement. She agreed to the adjustments and left feeling hopeful, despite all of the doom in gloom about the economy.

In 2009, Amy's investment account grew congruently with the DJIA, and she got a return of 17 percent. Her ending account balance in 2009, including her withdrawal of $22,000, was $133,398.

2010 was also another great year of recovery for the economy, and the stock market and her investment account yielded 10 percent, Factoring in her $22,000 withdrawal at the beginning of 2010, she finished the year with an account balance of $122,538.

In the beginning of 2011, Amy met with her adviser, and they filed the paperwork to turn on her guaranteed income stream of $39,397.45. She made it! She was now enjoying an income she could not outlive and enjoying more income in retirement than she really needed. She was happy and confident about her future.

The good times didn't stop there for Amy. As we all know, over the next seven years, the DJIA grew from 11,722 pts. to 19,855 pts. Amy had no need to touch her investment account during that time, and the value soared from $122,538 to $172,000, all while she was still receiving income from her fixed indexed annuity!

Even though Amy endured the same experiences as Bruce, her results were much different. Amy's success was the product of a little luck, in the form of an introduction to a reliable independent adviser. However, we should credit Amy for being open to meeting with a stranger to see what they could offer. Let's credit Amy for being proactive in taking charge of her financial future. Credit Amy for knowing good advice when she hears it.

Amy's story is a powerful example of the many stories I've heard from people who have walked the same path. These are the stories that drive my passion for helping more good people avoid the old construct of investing and enjoy the benefits of a plan that will utilize the best of the securities and the insurance world to work synergistically and produce strong results.

I believe everyone should have access to understandable education, fiduciary-based advice and transparency. Unfortunately, the average investor is completely fooled by the old paradigm of retirement planning, and the relationship they think they have with the person advising them. Investors have been fooled into thinking that they only have access to a quarterly report, they'll never understand a Morningstar Report, and their stockbroker or 401(k) representative has a fiduciary-based standard.

The industry has done an incredible job of disconnecting their clients from their investments and hiding the truth of what is available out there. Remember Bruce?

Do you remember how Bruce became disconnected because he didn't fully understand the financial jargon spewed at him? He felt disconnected because he didn't fully understand his quarterly reports. He trusted that his employer would choose plan administrators that offered the best investment choices, not fully understanding that administrators only offered the best investment choices they could access, rather than what was offered in the entire marketplace.

Bruce's disconnection and poor planning cost him the opportunity to participate in the gains of the DJIA from 2009 to today and left him with a largely diminished amount of money for his retirement. He could have avoided the calamities that happened to him. This is my hope for you too!

Your Personal Strategy Session

In this chapter, you learned the importance of being open to expanding your understanding of what retirement plans should really do for your life. There can be a vast difference in performance between the old paradigm of structuring retirement plans and what I just shared with you. The amount of enjoyment and your ability to freely pursue your dreams in retirement are greatly influenced by the decisions you make and the advice you follow.

Let's shatter the old paradigm of saving for retirement. You now know there is something better out there. You know you have access to simple reporting. You now know that you can access an independent fiduciary-based adviser who can bring you the best choices, in their evaluation, of what's available in the marketplace.

This is your call to action! You now have no excuse for not having these tools made available to you. You've worked hard to save the money you have. Now go find a trusted adviser who can provide these tools and increase the connection to your retirement savings. Increase your chances of a happy and fulfilling retirement.

THE WAR OVER YOUR THINKING

CHAPTER 7
THE TYPICAL RETIREMENT

> "There is only one success – to be able to
> spend your life in your own way."
> ~ Christopher Morley

We are the product of our parents and their experience has a dramatic impact on what our thoughts of retirement are. They are the product of The Great Depression, two world wars, many regional-world conflicts, a presidential assassination, increasing drug prices, changes in health insurance coverage, etc.

Retirement is a relatively new social experiment in America. A long retirement, lasting more than ten years is uncharted territory! We are literally making up the definition of life in retirement as we go and we are really just beginning to scratch the surface of educating the public with the most effective ways to not run out of money in retirement and, more important, have a fulfilling life in retirement.

Consider this: the life expectancy of someone born in 1930 was 59.7 years. In 1940, it was 62.9 years. For someone born in 1950, 68.2 years [3]. People born in 1930 have different concerns in retirement than those born in 1950.

The primary concern in retirement for people born in the 1930s was health and saving money for themselves and their family. Their generation lived in a world where you kept the same job for twenty-five to forty years, and you enjoyed a corporate pension. Enjoying a secure income in retirement was more common, because of corporate pensions. If the average person of that generation was able to retire between 1995 and 2000, times were relatively stable financially. Most of the heavy lifting of saving for retirement should have been completed, and the corporate pension with social security, gave a strong sense of security to Americans who retired at that time.

Living fifteen to thirty years in retirement wasn't really on the radar for this generation. In fact, retirement was typically short. Wealth and prosperity was not as great in retirement, compared to those born in the mid-to-late forties, fifties, and early sixties. We are reaping the benefits of the groundwork laid by the "Greatest Generation."

So let's take a look at the old paradigm of the traditional life in retirement. Because retirement was a relatively short-lived event, it has been shaped in a predictable way. Here's how I've come to see retirement being lived.

Current paradigm of retirement for most retirees:

1. Honeymoon
2. Staying At Home and Continuing Old Habits
3. Chasing The Feeling Of Being Full

Many people walking in this path are simply living life in retirement defined by what they are expected to do. Life fits within a box of expectations for many, and people are not encouraged to venture outside of that box.

Chasing Fulfillment

It's my experience, working with clients near or in retirement, few people realize they are walking the same exact path in retirement as their peers and those before them. People experience their journeys in retirement individually.

While, in fact, life in retirement often follows the same predictable path for virtually everyone. Let's break down, categorically, the path almost everyone unintentionally walks as they enter and live in retirement.

These categories will give you a baseline of understanding of each specific phase, how to manage them, and how retirees unknowingly walk the same path together.

CURRENT PARADIGM OF RETIREMENT FOR MOST RETIREES

The Honeymoon Stage   Staying At Home & Continuing Old Habits   Chasing The Feeling Of Being Full

The Honeymoon

Who doesn't like honeymoons? This is the period in retirement of elation that a person feels in the beginning stages of retirement. You've worked hard for thirty-five plus years, eaten peanut-butter-and-jelly sandwiches and done without new cars and expensive vacations to get here. It's time to celebrate!

You are excited to…actually…do…nothing! For the first time in a long time you don't have to listen to the alarm clock, attend Monday morning conference calls, indulge clients with lunch, meet your report deadlines, or answer calls until 5 p.m. Wow, it feels really good!

For 35 years, you've put off real rest and relaxation; good quality uninterrupted time with your spouse or your family; and playing. So, let's go play! You've been watching everyone else in retirement on the television for years.

Television advertisements depict retirees who are travelling, riding motorcycles, enjoying picnic birthday parties, and dancing, all the while pitching the newest pharmaceutical drug or shiny new object we should be buying. So what do you do? You do what everyone else does! You buy the new set of golf clubs, get a car for your spouse, take an expensive vacation, invite your family over for backyard picnics, and complete that remodel job you just can't put off any longer. After all, you have nowhere else to be.

The honeymoon is awesome! It seems like a perpetual vacation and party. Days slip into weeks and weeks slip into months, but retirees should beware! Beware of the restlessness you may begin to experience, typically in six to twelve months. Before we dig into the restlessness of retirement, let's spend some time looking into the type of honeymoon you may experience.

After thirty-five-plus years of having to keep a schedule, doing work-related things you probably didn't fully enjoy and dealing with difficult people, you're ready to have fun. The retirement honeymoon starts with a full appreciation of not having to be anywhere on anyone else's schedule, not needing to do things you don't really enjoy and not dealing with difficult personalities for the sake of work.

The first thing new retirees tell me they like to do is sleep in. They love getting up without an alarm clock and leisurely fixing breakfast. Doing anything that isn't racing off to work is a great feeling. They've worked their tail off. They deserve to pull back a little.

The next thing most newly retired people tell me they like to do is travel. They finally have the financial means and time to go explore for extended periods of time, without the threat of the "vacation" being over and having to go back to work. Planning an adventurous trip is exciting and feels like a well-deserved reward for making it to retirement.

It's so exciting to explore new places, travel to see family, and live an adventurous life. For some new retirees, taking a few vacations a year is enough to satisfy their sense of adventure. For others, it becomes a full-time occupation.

Many retirees have shared with me that they are done with delaying the kitchen remodel they've been putting off, buying their dream car, or not hitting the golf course numerous times a week. I love to hear when clients, especially those who have newly retired, visit me grinning ear-to ear and tell me about a purchase they've made, a project they are starting, or the greatest day on the golf course that they've put off for years or not been able to do. I'm sure it's much more relaxing to play golf on a Tuesday rather than fighting the crowds on a Saturday or Sunday.

What about family time with the kids and grandkids? We can't pass that up as a big benefit of being on the retirement honeymoon. The kids need a sitter for the grandkids. Grandma and Grandpa to the rescue! A grandchild in another state has a birthday coming up. Who's sending a birthday card? Not the new retirees. They are going to hand deliver the card, along with a couple of nice presents and a delicious birthday cake! Oh, it feels good not to have to work.

This is what I define as the retirement honeymoon. For some retirees, this lasts a month. For others, the honeymoon can last for years. Go ahead. Treat yourself. You deserve it.

Staying At Home And Continuing Old Habits

I'm sure anyone reading this book in retirement or preparing to retire just can't fathom staying at home in retirement. Why would you anyone want to stay at home when the cage door has just been opened, and you can do anything?

Well, many retirees who worked dedicated stressful careers with limited personal time often opt for "riding the recliner" in the early retirement months. I've worked with many new retirees who are just flat burned-out from their careers and schedules.

These are the dedicated professionals who were defined by their career and the accomplishments of their career. My favorite question for these people is, "now what?"

I can tell in an instant when someone has had a stressful career and endured working in situations with people they didn't like, because the answer is quick and precise. "Nothing!" sure seems to work well for the over-worked and underappreciated.

As the old saying goes, "old habits die hard. I've listened to many new retirees tell me how easy it is to stay in their old habits. They tell me they feel like they can get stuck in certain areas of their lives because they've "just done it that way" for so long.

Simple things like eating, exercise and watching a favorite television show seem to become more and more engrained for many retirees. Eating at a certain time and sitting down for the favorite show just seems to feel comfortable. Many retirees have expressed how hard it can be to form new habits because their old way of doing things keeps creeping into their lives.

It's easier to fall into a rut than you think. Think about it. Between the travelling, playing golf, exercising, and seeing family, there is a lot of down time. A lot! If you're not diligent in forming and practicing new habits, you will continue to do what you've been doing for the last thirty-five years. Don't worry, I'm going to give you strategies later in the book to choose and develop new habits in retirement.

Chasing Feeling Full

Chasing the feeling of being full is a dangerous trap. Many good people who don't properly plan their retirement or think about what they will experience emotionally and spiritually fall into this trap rather quickly. For most, the contentment from resting up and healing from years of hard work wears off after the first few months of retirement.

The mental challenge of work is gone. The excitement of growing professionally and overcoming day-to-day challenges is over, but it's not out of the new retiree's system. The body, mind, and soul are so conditioned to day-to-day challenges that once they receive proper rest, they crave the stimulation they once enjoyed. New retirees do get restless.

A quick and easy way to feed this restlessness is by chasing the feeling of being full. We think that if we scratch the itch of restlessness, it will go away, but it doesn't. We travel, we go to picnics, we check off milestones, and we buy new shiny objects, thinking that these distractions will help us scratch the itch.

Boy, does it feel good! It feels great to go on the balloon ride you always dreamed of, buy the car you've always wanted, travel to the beach you looked at in magazines for years. What could be better than playing golf with your spouse at the exclusive club mid-week? Does life get any better than when you get a new dining room set? Is there a better thrill in retirement than seeing the latest blockbuster movie?

Your Personal Strategy Session

I could go on and on and on, but I think you are starting to get the point. Each of these retirement milestones are fun to check off, but many people in retirement describe doing these things or buying new treats, enjoying them for a short time, and then thinking, "now what?"

Think of a child opening birthday presents. They all love getting presents. In fact, they'll take all you can give them, but do the toys really make them happy? Nope.

It will be no different for you either. The fun little secret is that you can have the temporary satisfaction of buying a shiny object AND you can find greater fulfillment in living a life true to who you really want to be. Have you thought about what that looks like for you? Go ahead, make a list…

6 PITFALLS IN RETIREMENT YOU MUST AVOID

> "To be prepared is half the victory".
> ~ Miguel de Cervantes

I'd like to share with you some of the key pitfalls I've seen people fall into after retiring. I believe that those who understand the circumstances, situations, and events they may encounter in retirement have a better chance of avoiding the snags and of feeling fulfilled in the third chapter of their life.

I've personally interviewed more than 1,000 retirees over the years, and I've observed retirees defaulting to a retirement lifestyle lacking excitement, positive challenges, contribution in significant ways, personal growth, and, ultimately, fulfillment. Below are a few of the pitfalls I've witnessed over the years.

- Little social interaction
- Feelings that the best days are behind and gone
- No valuable contribution to make
- Lack of real purpose

So how do people get caught up in these pitfalls instead of evolving in retirement for maximum fulfillment? In my experience, there are six circumstances, situations, and events that prevent retirees from moving forward in their retirement years.

- Lack of money
- Lack of permission
- Health complications
- Isolation
- Waiting for milestones
- Not feeling relevant or believing they have no value to offer

In my life, being aware of these thought patterns has helped me to continually push myself past the pitfalls of life, without getting stuck in a self-destructive rut. Let's unpack each of these scenarios, so that you can identify whether you are experiencing any of these thought patterns, and start on a path to self-correction.

1. Lack Of Money

Feeling like you lack financial resources can paralyze anyone. There are few things that frustrate me more professionally than watching good people get paralyzed by the feeling of not having enough.

It's easy to feel like we don't have enough financially in this day and age. Every time we turn on the television or log on to social media we are constantly bombarded by images of wealth and abundance that we can't access.

We are consumed by the fantasy that everyone around us is buying a new car, a beautiful house, or a fancy watch, or that they are constantly travelling and are feeling happy, happy, happy! It's easy to get caught up in the idea that we don't have enough when other people's abundance is constantly shoved in our face.

Rather than looking inward for personal satisfaction and happiness, we are constantly and subconsciously told we must measure our happiness in terms of our possessions or the events that take place in our lives.

This reminds me of a couple I worked with years ago. When I drove into the couple's property for a visit, I was immediately impressed. Their home sat at the base of the Flatirons Mountains in Boulder, Colorado. It was huge! As I was lead into their home, I couldn't help but be impressed at the size. (Did I mention that it was enormous?)

When I first sat down to talk to the couple in their kitchen, they seemed very happy, content and proud. They talked about their home, a lot, and I could tell they clearly showcased their home to impress guests. During my interview with them, the tone of our visit changed as we dug into their finances and unpacked who they really were.

I like to talk about more than just about money when I'm considering on taking new clients, to really get to know them. It's important for me to understand their hopes, dreams, and most importantly, any concerns or worries they have about their lives before and after retirement.

As I began to peel back the layers of their situation, I could feel their fear about something they seemed to have an abundance of...money. This couple had been living a lie for a long time. And they were desperate for help.

In reality, they had no money. The husband's employer had run into financial trouble, and the husband's pension was going to be dramatically reduced. They had taken investment advice from a neighbor who said he was getting huge returns from some investment strategy. They later discovered their neighbor was full of baloney. Unfortunately, they didn't make any changes to the investments before they experienced major losses.

It gets worse. They were renting their home, their furniture, and their cars, and they had a major spending problem. The couple was looking to me for help. Their lack of actual cash was making them miserable. Their lack of money, due to their decisions, had them home-bound, and they were beginning to isolate themselves from friends.

They wanted to get back to living a life true to themselves, but they were stuck because of their financial situation. Feeling broke had become paralyzing to them, and instead of working on their personal growth and development to find fulfillment, they were now anchored at home, worried about the future. Ultimately, we decided not to work together because they saw more value in keeping up appearances for the people around them than making necessary changes to feel more secure in life.

No matter how much money you believe you have or will make, if you are spending more than you are earning, you may very well find yourself in this situation. Being content with where you are and living within your means is both empowering and freeing. Don't be locked in a cage because of a lack of money.

2. Lack Of Permission

Feeling like you lack financial resources leads to the belief that you lack permission to follow your passions and live your life with confidence. Lacking permission to do the things you really want to do and pursue your interests is extremely frustrating.

A couple recently came to my office feeling frustrated. They had been clients of mine for about twelve months, and things were better for them financially than we had predicted. Their accounts had grown more than we had anticipated with the models we developed.

During our visit, they told me they had found their dream retirement home. It was only a few miles from their current home, but it had everything that they had dreamed of in a home. As they told me about the property, I couldn't help but notice the spark in their eyes and the excitement in their voices.

When they were done explaining the details of the property and all they could do with it, I told them I couldn't wait to see it. That's when the tone of the meeting changed. With a little embarrassment, humility, and wonder in their voices, they told me they didn't know if they could afford the extra cost of purchasing the property.

I watched their bodies and faces physically tighten as they explained their concerns about buying their dream retirement home. They had never explored the opportunity of purchasing this dream home because they felt the extra cost could put a strain on their retirement savings. No one had given them the financial permission and the confidence they needed to believe that they could live this retirement dream. Sounds kind of funny doesn't it? Grown adults feeling insecure about not having the permission to spend their own money. Don't laugh or judge. We all experience these insecurities.

This couple was in my office to get my permission that their retirement plan could handle the extra expense of buying their dream property. As we ran the hypothetical stress test models on their plan, I could see that they would be able to handle it.

I'll never forget the day they came into my office to review the results. They walked in looking serious and sat very straight in the chairs. As we reviewed the results of the stress tests, I was happy to report that I felt their retirement plan could handle the extra expense of purchasing their dream retirement home.

It was if a weight had been lifted from their shoulders. The tightness in their lips and chests disappeared instantly. My permission was met with a simultaneous sigh of relief and smiles on both of their faces.

I found the conversation we had before they left very interesting. It was fascinating to hear about how they felt paralyzed by a lack of permission to pursue their dream. The husband explained how they had almost just given up hope of going after their dream home because of their doubts. I'm so glad they had the courage to come visit me to explore the likelihood of their successfully purchasing the property and live their retirement dream to the fullest.

Helping my clients get what they truly want in retirement and pursue their passions is what rewards me the most. Whether I can give them that through doing a great job of delivering safe, consistent, returns or by just offering an encouraging word of permission makes all of the challenges of my profession worth it. I often wonder how many people don't fully live a life true to their dreams because they haven't heard a simple word of permission or encouragement to help them do so.

3. Health Challenges

Health problems don't happen to us, they happen to other people. I'll prove it to you. Do a little exercise for me. I want you to think about where you see yourself in five years. Picture where you are physically, whom you are with, the activity you are doing, the time of year it is, and what you both look like. What does this scene look like to you? How does it make you feel? What are the sounds you might hear? What are the smells hitting your nose? What taste is in your mouth in this scene? Take a moment a do this exercise. Breathe deeply and immerse yourself in your "happy place" to its fullest.

I guarantee you a couple of things. First, not one person doing this exercise will see themselves in the same place, with the same person, doing the same thing, at the same time of year as anyone else. Second, everyone will see themselves five years from now in the body they are in at this moment, with one exception. You won't be feeling any of the ailments or health challenges you currently have.

That's the rub. We don't like to admit or face our morbidity in life. No one likes to think that they will have anything less than perfect health. In fact, our health care professionals encourage us to think of ourselves as nothing less than healthy. It's never ceased to amaze me when I'm talking to a prospective client about their health.

I'll ask them where they think they fall on the health scale (unhealthy, decent health, very healthy). Without fail, almost everyone rates themselves on the very healthy scale. However, the truth comes out when I dig deeper into questions about their medications, surgeries, and doctor supervision.

They may have had a hip replacement a year ago, take high blood pressure medication, have hypothyroidism, or experience a touch of arthritis, but they will still say they are in great health. The reality is this is not very healthy person. So why do we live in such a state of denial? It's because the advancements of medical technology are helping people to live longer and with less limitations. But that doesn't mean that health challenges won't keep us from living the life we desire.

Case in point, I had some clients a couple of years back whom I was interviewing for long-term health care planning. We'll call them Barry and Julie Certa. I sat with this couple for more than thirty minutes as they explained to me how great their health was. They were very convincing, but I know better than to just take people at their word. Even though I explained how important it was to be truthful about their health history so that I could make the best recommendations possible and match them with the company that would give them the best chance for approval, I still knew I had to dig deeper. During the review of their application and medical history, they continued to affirm their health was in great shape.

I reviewed the health questions they would be asked on the application, and, not surprisingly, they answered "no" to every condition for which a person might need to get treatment from a doctor. I thanked them for their time and started to walk from the kitchen to the front door. Just as I was about to hit the tile in the foyer, something caught my eye. A thin plastic tube was lying next to the baseboard in the hallway. I quickly followed the plastic tube with my eyes, looking for where it led. Sure enough, the tubing continued down the hall and towards the master bedroom.

I turned to the husband and wife, who were close behind me, and asked what the plastic tube was for, even though I knew exactly what is was for. Barry just stared at me, not wanting to say anything, and Julie said, dismissively, "Oh, that's just for a little oxygen my husband needs from time to time".

Back to the kitchen table we went. I had to explain to Barry and Julie that using oxygen is not for someone in great health, and I asked why they hadn't mentioned the oxygen use forty-five minutes earlier. His response was, "Well, I do just fine on oxygen, and I don't go anywhere anyway. I'm in good health." With more questioning, I was able to uncover that the oxygen use wasn't needed occasionally, but constantly.

Wanting to find a solution to their problem, I asked more questions regarding their lifestyle and activity level. The statement, "Well, I do just fine on oxygen, and I don't go anywhere, anyway," was ringing in my head. The truth of the matter was that Barry and Julie were homebound in retirement because of his health condition. They had no exercise routine, no hobbies other than television watching, and limited interaction with friends. Barry was the person using the oxygen, not Julie.

I asked the couple how the health complications affected their daily lives, and they said it had affected their relationship, happiness, and outlook on life. Barry and Julie were stuck in retirement doing the same day-to-day routine because of health complications.

Julie pitied Barry, because of his need for supplemental oxygen. Barry didn't like the pity. In fact, it really frustrated him, but he was extremely grateful to have such a dedicated spouse and partner. It affected their happiness because they couldn't travel the way they wanted and do all of the things they wanted to do.

Both of them were not optimistic about their future in retirement. In fact, they both felt cheated that they weren't able to live their dreams in retirement because of Barry's health. They wanted more. They never imagined living retirement imprisoned in their home by health. I left that interview extremely grateful for my health, and, more importantly, the dedication I have to the things that I can control about my health. Life is fragile, and we never know when things we can't control will change our intentions about life in an instant, or slowly, over time.

4. Isolation

How could isolation ever be a problem in retirement? Let's think about this for a second. What's the one thing many of us want to do at the end of a long workday? We want to be alone. Well, maybe not totally alone, but we want to either be with our spouse or our immediate family, certainly not with a crowd of people. Being a little isolated from the rest of the world seems like a holiday for many of us.

I'm sure there have been times in your life, sitting at your work desk, that all you can think about is getting away from it all. It's healthy to have a little isolation. Being isolated helps us to decompress, rejuvenate our physical and mental energy and to gain the mental clarity we need to solve problems we are experiencing.

However, extended isolation, with little social interaction, has been well documented, in multiple studies throughout the world, to increase the risk of cardiovascular problems, rheumatoid arthritis, osteoporosis, some forms of cancer, depression, and memory loss.

Isolated individuals are up to 50 percent more likely to develop cognitive decline. They are less likely to exercise, eat right, and develop hobbies. Compared to people who have regular social interactions, isolated individuals are more likely to need long-term health care and to be victims of elder abuse.

Many retirees fall into isolation by no fault of their own. Here's a list of circumstances to be aware of that can cause isolation.

- Financial changes in retirement
- Friends moving away
- Getting stuck in old daily habits
- Loss of optimism about the future
- Hearing loss
- Loss of mobility caused by health complications
- Grief resulting from loss of a spouse or close friend
- Physical and emotional pain
- Decreased sense of personal safety
- Problems with memory recall

I highly doubt that people ever anticipate how deeply isolation can affect their life in retirement. It's my hope, for you, that your new awareness of the negative effects of isolation helps you to avoid it in any shape or form.

5. Waiting For Milestones

We love to measure our progress in life by hitting milestones. Milestones are the measuring stick we use to analyze our progress in life, compare ourselves to others, and fit into the construct of the life we believe we should be living at the time we are living it. It is interesting to me that so much emphasis is actually put on milestones in life.

It's hard not to have our lives dictated by milestones. From the time we are infants we hear statements like:

When you're old enough you can...
When you graduate high school you can...
When you go to university you are a....

When you get married…
When you buy your first house…
When you have your first child…
When you have your second child…
When you are xxx years old…

We could go on and on with these statements. The point is milestones have been a part of our lives from the time we were infants. They are deeply ingrained in us. I can see how easy it is to measure life in terms of milestones, given the way we've been taught to get past them or to want to fulfill what others expect of us.

Milestones are an important part of human growth and development because they do give us feedback if we are on track, behind, or need help with our own growth and development. A few examples of retirement milestones are:

Age 59 ½ - This is the first time you can take distributions from an individual retirement account titled in your name without a 10 percent early withdraw penalty.

Age 62 - This is the age we can take our first elected Social Security payment.

Age 65 – This is the age you are eligible to enroll in Medicare health plans.

Age 66 to 67 – This is the full retirement age for Social Security. For many Americans, this is the age they may be able to receive their check with no reductions. Currently, if you were born between 1943 and 1954, your full Social Security retirement age is 66. If you were born in 1960 or later, your full Social Security retirement age is 67. For individuals born between 1955 and 1959, your full Social Security retirement age is somewhere between 66 and 67.

Age 70 – This is the age you are eligible for your maximum Social Security benefit. If you've delayed collecting Social Security until this age, you have been enjoying the maximum 8 percent increase in your check since the time you elected to suspend payments (elected at ages 66 to 67). There is no advantage for delaying your Social Security payments beyond this age.

Age 70 ½ - This is the age that you are required to take Minimum Distributions (RMDs) from your tax-deferred retirement accounts. For individuals turning age 70 ½, they must take and report their RMDs before April 1 of the year following the year they turned age 70 ½ . For example, if you turned age 70 ½ on September 1 of 2017 you must take your RMD by April 1, 2018.

Every RMD in a subsequent year must be taken by December 31 of that year. The penalty for failure to take your RMD at the correct time is 50 percent of the RMD amount. You don't want to miss this milestone!

So these milestones seem pretty positive in our lives. How in the heck can they hurt or prevent a person from having the most fulfillment in retirement? Quite simply, they can be the reason we put off doing important things now. But wait, isn't that a good thing? Mmmm…not necessarily.

CAUSES OF ISOLATION FOR RETIREES

- Financial changes in retirement
- Friends moving away
- Getting stuck in old daily habits
- Loss of optimism about the future
- Hearing loss
- Loss of mobility caused by health complications
- Grief resulting from loss of a spouse or close friend
- Physical and emotional pain
- Decreased sense of personal safety
- Problems with memory recall

Unfortunately, there are way too many stories of people passing away, leaving a spouse and family behind with regret. It hurts me when I hear about families who didn't take the full family trip, a person who didn't chase their childhood passion, and the story of how so-and-so always wanted to but never did x, y, or z.

Here are a few examples of negative milestones in retirement.

Children's Milestones – These are very dangerous traps! Have you ever heard someone say, or have you thought to yourself, "When my child finally does "x," we are all going to take a family trip. "X" can be a move, a job promotion, a wedding, a divorce, the birth of a grandchild, a work promotion, or an advanced degree. Beware, what if Johnny isn't motivated to accomplish "x" or just can't quite get it? You'll never take that trip. What would be more important to you, making family memories on a vacation or waiting for Johnny to accomplish something you don't have control of? Trust me…it's the memories and connection that are much more important in the long run.

Personal Health Milestones – Personal health milestones are very tricky. For couples in retirement, they can affect a spouse as much as the person who is experiencing the personal health problems. I believe it's very important for all of us to have the courage to face the reality of our own good and poor health. It's important because if we have the courage to face the reality of our situation, it can help us to make important decisions about delayed gratification of experiences, events, and opportunities.

At the time of my mother's passing in 2016, I didn't have the courage to face her mortality. We had plenty of time to talk about her health, but we didn't because I always thought she would get better and that I would have time to talk to her about the "important stuff" if things really got bad.

Can you imagine? We had every opportunity to talk about real meaningful subjects, but let the time and opportunities slip by. We could have really shared some heart to heart moments and deepened our connection, but we didn't because we denied her health situation and we lacked the courage to share our thoughts and feelings with each other. I honestly kept thinking "Mom is going to feel better after this treatment, and we'll talk about <insert topic> then, or I'll take her <here> when she feels better." The really frustrating thing is, even though we did many great things together the summer she passed, I didn't have the courage to engage her in real, meaningful conversation because I was waiting for a health milestone that never came.

If you are thinking or have heard a person you care about say they are waiting for their own, or their spouses' health to improve before they talk about something on their mind or visit a place they been wanting to go to, please encourage them not to wait. Go do what you are waiting to do, now, to the best of your ability, at this very moment.

Even though a health challenge may keep you from physically doing all that you want to do, do whatever you can. Go have the heart to heart talk you've been planning on having. Pursue your secret passion. Take your loved one to that special place. It's more important you do it now rather than wait for your health to be perfect. It may never be!

6. I Have Nothing Of Value To Contribute. I'm Not Relevant

Feelings of inadequacy and low self-esteem affect many retirees. It can be hard to find relevance in the age of super-computers for many retirees. The computer age has passed many retirees by, and it continues to be picking up steam. In a time when twenty-somethings have hundreds of thousands and millions of followers and "friends" on Twitter, Snapchat, YouTube, and Facebook, how can retirees not feel left behind in some ways? How can they find relevance in the modern age?

Is it possible that when a retiree hits age 65, they've hit their expiration date? Is it possible that retirees have used up their value and have nothing more to offer? Lee Iacocca revealed in *Wired*, "I've always been against automated chronological dates to farm people out. The union would always say, 'Make room for the new blood; there aren't enough jobs to go around.'

We all know that people don't suddenly lose the talent and experience gained over a lifetime with passing of a birthday. But, somehow we are expected to believe that the world has outpaced our knowledge and experience. We're told through media channels that the "new" is what is relevant. Experience is irrelevant.

Employment opportunities for people near retirement seem to be few and far. The recession of 2009 caused many companies to really look at their balance sheets and find ways to streamline their budgets. To many companies, after 2009, the senior employees are not seen as an advantage for their wisdom, work ethic, and commitment, but they were seen as an expensive salary liability on the corporate balance sheet. Decisions were made to cut the more expensive and experienced employees and many good people near retirement lost their jobs. Corporations opted for more inexperienced and cheap young labor. Do you know anyone near retirement after 2009 who got "downsized"? Yep. Me too… many.

According to the Department of Labor, in December of 2012, people age 55 and older spent an average of 52.2 weeks unemployed and more than 210,000 others quit looking all together. Those people will tell you about the difficulties of finding employment so close to retirement.

Many Americans in this situation may feel that they are irrelevant and have nothing of value to contribute in the fast-changing age of technology. The prospect of having to reinvent and learn new skills is frustrating for many people because even if they get more training and education, there will still be a mark against them on their application… age.

This spills over into retirement. Imagine the psyche of a person who was downsized because of age, just prior to retirement. Would you feel as if the skill set you sharpened for thirty-plus working years meant anything in retirement? Would you have a great sense of relevance in the world having been forced into retirement by a corporate downsize?

The truth is that retirees have more value than they think. Just because it doesn't fit into the traditional construct of how value is measured doesn't mean it doesn't matter. Finding new value in your experience will require a shift in thinking.

Your Personal Strategy Session

Try thinking of retirement in a different way. Think of retirement as a time in your life to explore new options. Don't think of it as a time to put your skills out to pasture. Are there creative ways that you can apply your skills outside of corporate America? Do charities in your community need someone with your skill set to help the cause? Can you turn your skill set into a hobby that keeps you energized intellectually and emotionally? Is there a way that you can use your skills doing something you never get tired of?

Just a small shift in your thinking can help you find relevance and value in retirement. The beauty of this period in your life is that you can find value and relevance on your schedule, at your pace. You now have the time to explore and play. This is when you can discover how the skills you obtained and sharpened in your career apply to your perfect world, as opposed to the corporate world.

Let's look at how a typical retirement plays out. Please follow me through a story that I've witnessed many times in various ways.

CHAPTER 8
MARK AND MARGARET'S RETIREMENT STORY

The Typical Retirement Journey

Mark and Margaret have been married for forty-plus years. Like many Americans born in the 1930s, Mike got a good job at the start of his working years for a local company. It didn't pay a lot, but it did pay enough for Mark to support Margaret and their three small children.

Mark made up for the average pay by working long hours. Margaret worked hard managing the house and raising their three children. Mark had to endure the trade-off of providing for his family by working eight to ten hours a day. He missed many of his kids' school accomplishments and sports competitions in order give his family a "good life." Family vacations consisted of trips camping or visiting relatives.

Margaret had to experience the trade-off of managing the household and raising three children while also working ten to twelve hours a day. She worked tirelessly at home alone. She did her best to keep the house "on budget" and happy. All of the hard work really paid off. Mark was exceling at his job. The kids all successfully made it into college and graduated. They lived close to home, working jobs of their own. Everyone was happy.

What Mark and Margaret didn't realize was that while they were busy making a living, they were losing small pieces of themselves. Mark and Margaret didn't have time to pursue or develop new hobbies. Their kids were their hobbies. Often, when the day was done, Mark and Margaret had only just enough energy to enjoy some television together. The weekends were spent doing household chores. Sunday was the one day the family could have fun together.

Over the years, the exhausting work and long hours begin to talk their toll. Mark became overweight because he didn't have time to exercise, and he lost control over his diet, because of client lunch and dinner commitments. Mark developed type 2 diabetes and hypertension at the age of 55.

Margaret also started feeling the effects of being a homemaker. The constant grind of daily chores, worrying about keeping everyone "on track", managing the household budget, and trying to keep everyone happy contributed to Margaret being diagnosed with stage I breast cancer and arthritis at 57.

Thankfully, Mark successfully managed his type 2 diabetes and hypertension with medication, but his health continued to slow him down, and he continued to gain weight. Margaret successfully treated and beat her diagnosis of stage I breast cancer, but her arthritis continued to advance.

Mark and Margaret were able to decrease their working schedules in the last five years of Mark's working career. They were both looking forward to Mark's retirement at age 65. His company was providing Mark a pension, equal to 75 percent of his last year working with the company. Social Security benefits would make up the difference, and it looked like Mark will have very little change in income during retirement.

In the last two years of his career, Mark had a mini-stroke, at age 63. Luckily, there were no residual side effects from the mini-stroke, but Mark had an awakening about his own mortality. After his recovery, he dedicated more time to thinking about what he'd like to do with his wife Margaret in retirement.

At retirement, Mark's type 2 diabetes required daily injectable treatment. His blood pressure, although controlled, was still a reason for concern. Margaret seemed to be faring well with her arthritis, but she was scheduled to see a specialist about a hip replacement.

So how did this chain of events affect Mark and Margaret's retirement dreams? Significantly, that's how. Mark and Margaret realized that their health wasn't the best, and they were worried because they'd seen long-time friends die within five years of retiring.

Mark and Margaret were caught in the retirement trap. Retirement had become, for Mark and Margaret, one event after another, with no thoughts of personal growth. They thought retirement was when they would make up for lost time and do the things they delayed in life while they were younger, more mobile, and healthier, but they can't. They are simply reacting to life as it is happening to them. It's what I refer to as the event of retirement.

Here's how I've seen how these retirements play out. Mark and Margaret are so relieved that they've made it to retirement that they start having fun. The first year of retirement, Mark and Margaret do what most other fresh retirees do. They start checking of their retirement bucket list.

Much of the first few months of retirement are spent doing nothing. Both enjoy the fact they really have no place to be. They spend the mornings waking up later than usual, reading the paper, and thinking about home remodeling. They plan a few trips to visit relatives and take a beach vacation.

Mark and Margaret spend the next year occupying their time traveling to their kids and grandkids birthday parties, indulging in their favorite television shows, driving from one dinner with friends to the next dinner with friends, and managing their health the best they can. Sound familiar?

Three years into retirement Mark begins to get restless. He is feeling like he needs to do more. You see, Mark has always had this itch in the back of his head. It's an itch he starts feeling that needs to be scratched. Ever since Mark was young, he loved fishing, especially fly-fishing. He never had the time to pursue fishing when he was working because he had responsibilities. Family and work responsibilities pushed his passion for fly-fishing to the end of the line... *literally.*

Putting his passion on hold never really bothered him, because he got a lot of fulfillment providing a great life for his family and being an expert in his role at work. When he was younger and thought about fishing, he would picture himself fly-fishing either in a beautiful mountain river or on the salt-water flats of Florida. The funny thing is that, when Mark was imagining himself fishing, he always imagined himself in each environment as a young man in his 30s or 40s, never as the person he had become.

Mark decides that now is the time to pursue his childhood passion of fishing. He starts to read about the new tackle available and places close to him where he can fish. Within a month, he hires a guide to teach him how to scout for fish and cast with the correct lures. Mark is in heaven! He's finally living his dream of fishing. As time goes on, Mark's fishing guide encourages him to hike into areas close to him for better fishing. That's when it hits Mark. He doesn't have the wind, the strength, or the balance he used to have for hiking. The diabetes is having an effect on his body he never imagined.

Now the idea of hiking to his dream areas to fish is compromised. Not easily discouraged, Mark starts thinking about taking some trips to fish in the salt-water flats of Florida...and then IT happens.

One week before Mark's first trip to Florida, Margaret has a bad fall. She was getting groceries out of the car, tripped on her shoelace, and falls hip-first on the concrete. Screaming in pain, she's calling for Mark.

After thirty minutes, Mark finally hears the cries for help from his wife coming from the garage. He races in to find her on the concrete and calls 911. Margaret is rushed to the hospital and gets the news that she has shattered her hip. Further tests reveal that she is suffering from advanced osteoporosis and is at a high risk for more broken bones.

As any good spouse would, Mark cancels all of his fishing plans to Florida. Margaret requires around the clock help recovering from her hip replacement. They have no children living within sixty miles, and they don't want to inconvenience their friends by asking them to stay with Margaret just so Mark can go fishing.

Mark is homebound with his wife, and they both are hoping for better days. They spend their days together, playing cards, watching television, and planning their first trip when Margaret fully recovers. Mark continues to add to his waistline. His diabetes is worsening, and neuropathy begins to develop. They are both feeling restless but are waiting for a good bill of health from the doctor and don't really feel an urgency to start pursuing their passions. After all, they expect to live well into their eighties and nineties. They feel like they have plenty of time ahead of them.

After six months of rest and therapy, Margaret gets the green light from her physician to get back to her normal life. The happy couple packs their bags for a trip to Florida. They plan on walking the beach and touring the shops together.

They spend their first day strolling the shops, taking a short half-mile walk on the beach and having a delicious dinner together. On the second day, Margaret notices Mark is limping and can't seem to walk his normal pace. His neuropathy is slowing him down, and his extra weight is decreasing his stamina. Not to worry his wife, Mark brushes his difficulties off on the heat.

Mark and Margaret have waited a long time for this trip, and Mark really wants to do everything he can with his wife. On day three, Mark pushes himself in the heat. Tired from the walking throughout the day, Mark misses a curb on the way to the car. He falls and hits his head on the concrete. The injury to Mark's head is so severe that he dies in the hospital two days later from complications.

This is a tragic, horrible story! Unfortunately, it's much more common than people think. You may know of a family who has endured a similar set of events in their life.

There are some lessons to be learned from Mark and Margaret's story. Let's break it down into the retirement ladder I described earlier.

The Retirement Phases:

Honeymoon
Stay At Home
Continuing Old Habits
Chasing The Feeling Of Being Full (Play Play Play)

Mark and Margaret enjoyed the Honeymoon Phase, sleeping late and over-indulging in television, lunches, dinners, and having no schedule. It was nice to not have any place to be, so for a few months, it was great to stay at home and catch up on some projects, relax, read, and just be with each other.

Being content with staying at home and having no place to be contributed to their lack of desire to make new schedules, develop new routines, and try new things. They were comfortable with each other. They were just enjoying being and having no "have-tos". They didn't "have to" be at work at a certain time, eat lunch at a scheduled time, or to attend late-night meetings. Staying at home helped them to continue their old habits. Who wouldn't fall into this trap? Many retirees unknowingly fall right into this trap.

No one had talked to, or with Mark and Margaret, about the unseen obstacles and events in retirement that cause good people to lead an unfulfilling retirement. Even if the circumstances in the preceding story remain unchanged, I do believe it's possible that Mark and Margaret would have made different choices about the retirement they would choose to live.

Hopefully, you can see how health can dramatically affect our experience in retirement. Mark's story has come to an end, but there is more to Margaret's story.

THE PHASES OF RETIREMENT

Honeymoon Stage

Enjoying being at home

Continuing Old Habits

Chasing The Feeling
Of Being Full

Your Personal Strategy Session

Has a situation like this ever happened to you or someone you know?

How has the situation impacted your life or the life of the people around you?

Do you see how easy it is to get caught reacting to the circumstances in life with little control?

Have you ever been a victim of reacting to life with little control?

How does a person in this situation find the motivation and direction to reshape their new life?

Would a guidebook help the process of reshaping life without a life partner or loved one?

CHAPTER 9
MARGARET'S JOURNEY CONTINUES

After Mark's death, Margaret understandably struggles in many ways. For the first time in her life, she has to be responsible for understanding her finances and must endure completing the required financial paperwork caused by her husband's passing. While struggling with her loss, in the fog of depression, Margaret has to meet with the person handling her family's finances.

She feels so inadequate because she doesn't understand the language that is being used in the meetings and doesn't even understand why all of the paperwork has to be filed. After all, it's "their" money. Frustrated and depressed about her situation, she becomes disconnected from her finances and accepts the situation. After all, the person helping her to complete the paperwork says, "Everything is going to be OK".

Things are OK financially for Margaret. Thankfully, she sees no change in her finances, except that her accounts now only bear her name.

As time goes by over the next six months, life gets back to normal for the rest of the family. The children are refocused on their lives, and Margaret is finding her own emotional strength. She feels most comfortable in her home, alone.

Still dealing with the depression of losing her life partner, Margaret is struggling with the desire to reach out to friends and continue those connections. She doesn't want to bother them or waste their time, and she doesn't call her children, in fear that they will worry about her. She unconsciously does what many people in her situation do. She begins to isolate herself.

Mark was her life. They did everything together. They did everything for each other. The kids are grown and independent, and she feels that no one needs her like Mark did. She just can't shake her depression or find things to do without Mark.

As time slowly passes, her depression and isolation only get worse. She is struggling because of a lack of a heartfelt connection to others. Her depression continues to isolate her, and she doesn't have the courage to talk to family and friends because they have their own lives to live.

She stays at home sewing and knitting and takes comfort in the soothing repetition of the needle and thread. Sewing and knitting help Margaret to take her mind off of her isolation and lack of connection.

After a year, Margaret notices her arthritis is becoming more and more uncomfortable. The pain that started in her hands has now progressed to her knees.

She visits her arthritis specialist and they increase her medication, but her range of motion is decreasing.

The arthritis is now effecting her sewing and knitting. Her hands just don't have the endurance and ease of movement she used to. Stitches and patterns she used to complete with ease are now becoming increasingly difficult. She is becoming increasingly frustrated with her hands.

During a phone conversation with her mother, Margaret, Sarah notices that her mother beginning to repeat herself uncharacteristically. This concerns her, because as she is thinking about the conversation, she takes a mental inventory of past conversations, and things begin to add up. This isn't the first time Margaret has done this, but it is the first time that Sarah really noticed.

As Sarah is talking with her husband about her concerns for Margaret, he too says he's noticed that she repeats herself, but he hasn't given it much thought. Concerned, Sarah travels to Margaret's home to pay her a visit.

Sarah arrives at home and is ready to spend some good family time with her mother. As she walks through the door with her bag, Margaret is dressed nicely with a big smile on her face, excited for her daughter to visit. They give each other a big warm hug and Margaret says to Sarah, "You must be thirsty from the drive. Let's get you some water." They walk in the kitchen to grab a glass of water and catch up.

Sarah is sipping on her water talking to her mother, who is sitting at the kitchen table. Everything looks normal. There are no dishes in the sink. The sink is clean. The floor is swept. The dishtowel is folded next to the sink as normal. Conversation is normal.

Sarah finishes her water and puts the glass in the dishwasher. They sit at the kitchen table together, relaxing and talking about the grandkids. Margaret is so happy to have her daughter visiting. She is smiling, relaxed, and happy and so is Sarah.

"Can I get you a glass of water, dear?" says Margaret. "You must be thirsty from your drive." Sarah replies, "No Mom. I'm OK. I already had some water."

"Oh, how silly of me," responds Margaret. Margaret starts to gets up from the table and Sarah sees how difficult it is for her mother to stand up quickly. Margaret has to put both hands on the table and does her best not grimace and stands with a smile. "Oh, my aching knees. I'm just not what I used to be." Margaret says dismissingly.

They walk to the front room where Sarah left her bag, and Margaret turns and says,

"Let's get you unpacked. I'm so excited to have you home. Your room is all ready." Sarah grabs her bag and heads up the stairs, but Margaret doesn't follow.

As she unpacks her bags, she takes a mental inventory of the bedroom. Thankfully, everything looks tidy and in order. There's nothing to be concerned about. It looks like Mom is keeping everything together. She is relieved.

Sarah walks down the stairs, and finds Margaret sitting in her favorite chair reading a book. "Mom, how's your knitting coming? Have you been trying any new stitches", she asks. "No, I'm afraid my arthritis is getting the best of me these days, and I just can't knit for any length of time", Margaret shares. "So what are you doing to keep yourself busy, Mom", asks Sarah.

"Well, I mostly read and watch my shows on television. You know I have my favorite shows to watch", says Mom. "Have you seen the Carlson's or the Ziegler's lately, Mom?" Margaret replies, "Yes, I see them about once a month. They're really busy, and I don't like to bother them, but they're doing great. Can I get you a glass of water, sweetie, you must be thirsty from your drive?"

Now Sarah is concerned. This is the third time Margaret has asked her the same exact question in sixty minutes. "No Mom. I'm alright," Sarah says with a smile on her face. "Mom, how are you doing? Are you OK? I really love you, and I know it must be difficult to be here alone. I don't want…We don't want you to be lonely. Is everything alright?" Sarah asks, sitting next to her Mom in the family room.

Margaret confides in her daughter, "Sarah, ever since Dad died, I've been doing my best not to bother anyone. You all have your own lives. You're all so busy and doing so well. I'm fine. I just don't feel like there is anything for me to do, and no one really needs me." She continues, "My friends are all so busy with their families and travelling it's just really hard to connect. Sometimes they invite me over, but I just don't feel up to it. Either my knees hurt, and I don't want to go anywhere, or I think there offering out of pity. I don't want to be a bother."

"Well, why don't we get you out, Mom? How about we plan a trip together? Where's a place you've always wanted to go? Let's go there? How about it? I've got some time next month, we can get away for a long weekend, Mom," Sarah says, doing her best to motivate her mother. "Oh no, honey. I'm just not feeling up to it these days, and besides, I don't want to spend the money, I can't afford it", says Margaret.

"Mom, you have plenty of money. Don't worry about it. Let's go," Sarah says enthusiastically. "No, no, sweetie," Margaret says, dismissing Sarah. "That money is for you and your brothers." Sarah objects, "What do you mean, Mom? We are doing just fine. It's your money. Let's go travel, that's what you have your money for."

Margaret dismisses Sarah again, "No. No. I already told you. I'm saving that money for you all." She stands up walks a few feet. Turns around and says with a smile, "Can I get you a glass of water sweetie, you must be thirsty from your drive?".

Unfortunately, many of you can connect with this story. I've heard this story many times in the interviews I've conducted over the years. Let's review what Margaret is dealing with as a widow.

She's having trouble reconnecting with family and friends after the passing of her husband. She doesn't want to be a bother. Margaret's health is deteriorating, and her knee problems prevent her from getting out of the house.

She's feeling isolated because of this and can't shake her depression. Her arthritis is slowly robbing her of her passion for sewing and knitting, and rather than create or follow other interests, she fills her time with the TV. Although she doesn't verbalize it to Sarah, she chooses not to get involved in the community because she feels irrelevant and has nothing to offer.

Margaret is similar to many retirees in the regard that, rather than using her money as a tool to improve her life, she has given up on the excitement of pursuing something new and feels her children's lives are more important than hers, so she decides it's better to leave as much of her money possible to the children, rather than using it for things she's interested in.

Her isolation from the community has caused her to think there is no way she can help others, because it's hard to even help herself. She has no responsibility to others and gets no fulfillment from contributing to her family, friends, or community.

Margaret's life has become boring to her. It feels like the same day repeated over and over.

Her world and comfort zone have been shrunk to the confines of her house. She feels comfortable there, and her pain is an excuse not get out an explore new connections with people who have the same interests as she does, or to visit places that she has been curious about or interests she's wanted to explore. She is reacting to life. She is reacting to her health. She is reacting to her emotions.

Truthfully, I can understand how people like Margaret get caught up in a life like this. I have complete empathy for her situation. I hope you can understand why I said earlier that we think retirement is its own unique experience. It is, but if you've connected with the story of Mark and Margaret, you can understand how we all really share the same experiences broken down the way we have just explored.

My singular wish for the creation of this book is to help people identify and avoid the pitfalls of retirement that lead retirees down the path of the old retirement paradigm. It's my sincerest hope, that what we are about to explore next, will inspire as many people to take control of their lives in retirement, empower them to gain as much control of the circumstances that happen to people in retirement and redirect their lives into a path of fulfillment, contribution, and connection.

Your Personal Strategy Session

<u>**Take out a notepad and write your thoughts pertaining to the questions below.**</u>

Have you ever given thought to what your life might look like after the loss of a life partner or loved one?

Think of 3 things about that person that would impact how you would live your life in their absence.
i.e. In honor of the memory of _____ I will always live my life focused on (what).

Would you seize the opportunity to do things you've been putting off?
Can you name 3 things you've been putting off that you should do now with or without a life partner?
What's been holding you back from completing the things you've been putting off?

Would an introduction of your financial adviser to your family be helpful?

Would a financial review be helpful for the survivors to be prepared for the day you are no longer on this planet?

Can you muster the courage to shake up your daily habits and reshape your life in the direction you want to take it now?

Have you thought about what you might do when the day comes you physical capabilities are not what they are now?

What activity might you do to keep you looking forward to a new day and excited about life when that time comes?

What obstacles are in the way of living a life that *YOU* really want?

AWAKENING

CHAPTER 10
6 OBSTACLES STANDING IN YOUR WAY

> "Action may not always bring happiness; but there is no happiness without action."
> ~ Benjamin Disraeli

We are often victims of our own choices and life circumstances…

In Bronnie Ware's 2009 online article titled "Regrets of the Dying," Bronnie reveals the insight she gained from having worked as a palliative caregiver. She talks about the close relationships she developed with her clients in the remaining weeks of their lives through "raw, honest conversations about life and death, including what the patients wished they had done differently."

From her experience, the number-one regret people had as they looked back on their lives was,

> I wish I'd had the courage to live a life true to myself, not the life others expected of me.

Isn't that strange? We have all of the tools before us to live a life in any way we wish. Each day that we wake up, we have a unique opportunity to be our true selves.

We have a unique way of creating our own reality through our minds and the expectations of others. For some, it's a small prison, and for others, it's a world of unlimited opportunities and potential. The daily choices we make directly influence our reality, and it's easy to take time for granted when we are in good health.

Being in good health can distract us from going out there and being true to who we really want to be. When we are healthy, there is no sense of urgency to go after our dreams or be true to ourselves because there is not much of a threat of opportunity loss. After all, bad health problems that cause limitations don't happen to us. They happen to other people. We aren't the ones who get sick. That happens to our neighbor.

Remember the visualization exercise I had you do earlier in the book? Imagine yourself five years from now, doing what you'd love to be doing. Imagine where you are, what the weather is like, whom you are with, what it feels like, etc. I bet you still are picturing yourself in your body as it is now, not what it will be five years from now. The point is we believe we are invincible... until that moment when we are not.

That moment you realize your health is a challenge, it may be too late. It may be too late because you can't walk the distance you thought you could. It may be too late because you can't physically travel like you used to. It may be too late because you don't have the strength you once had. Don't take your health for granted; it's an essential key to pursing ALL of your dreams.

So what could possibly prevent us from living a life that is true to ourselves? Talking with my clients and peers over the years, I've discovered other factors that limit our willingness to live a life true to ourselves. Here are a few others:

> "You can't help getting older, but you don't have to get old."
> ~ George Burns

Familial Expectations/Constructs

From the time we are children, the web of being "who we are supposed to be" is spun around our very existence. Our parents and the media show us, from a very young age, who we are supposed to be and how we should behave as children, teenagers, young adults, and adults. We are given the permission to act inside the confines of what it means to be a member of our family, our religion, our community, and our employer, etc. Acting outside of those confines is not often encouraged.

The web spun around us acts as a cocoon to insulate us from emotional or physical harm. Our parents create our emotional and physical cocoons because they want to save us from as much pain as possible. It's natural, and we all do it. In order to do that, carefully crafted boundaries and expectations are constructed and taught to us daily. If you want "x", you will do "y". When we are in public, we do "x". We never do "y". As members of "x" faith, we don't do "y". You get the idea.

Thankfully, we have people around us who are looking out for our welfare, as we are trying to figure out the game of life. I don't know about you, but I'd rather have someone helping me avoid the pitfalls of life, rather than running into them at full speed.

But wait…cocoons are for children. You've spent your life growing your independence and expanding your comfort zones. Aren't we trying to emerge from those cocoons? Heck yes.

So why are retirees expected to follow life's rules and expectations in retirement? Let's review them. Do these sound familiar?

"Mom, you're retired, don't saddle yourself with responsibility."
"Dad, you're too old to take up basketball at age 80."
"Grandma, you've had a hip replacement, you can't do a yoga workout."
"Dad, you've got nothing better to do, can you watch the grandkids four days a week in the afternoons?"
"You can pick up the dinner tab for the family. You're retired."

We can go on and on about the silly expectations family puts on retirees to help them feel more comfortable about how retirees are living and spending their time.

The difficult thing for all of us is to not let these expectations limit us as retirees. It's OK to give yourself permission to say "no" to these expectations and be a little selfish about the way you want to live your life. You've endured the delayed gratification of doing the things you really want to do to this point. You've earned it. The difficult thing to do is to swim upstream and live a life true to yourself, as Bronnie Ware discovered as a palliative caregiver.

> "Man is free at the moment he wishes to be."
> ~ Voltaire

Societal Pressures

We have an instinctive need to want to fit into our surroundings. This affects some of us more than others. It's commonly known as keeping up with the Joneses. If fitting in means that we'll dress alike, eat the same foods, have the same accent, and behave the same way in public, then that's what we do. As humans, we are constantly looking for affirmations that we fit in. Why do you think the television and social media have such an influence on our everyday lives? Those two entities capitalize on our instinctive need to fit in by telling us, exactly, how and what we need to do to be "in the moment."

They tell us the types of clothes we should wear, the vacations we should take, how we should think about ourselves in retirement, the drugs we should take and even the types of personal care products we should use. So, how does that relate to us living a life true to ourselves?

There are countless people who have sacrificed what they really wanted to be in life because of societal pressures and expectations. I'll use my own life as an example.

Throughout my life, I've always wanted to make a big difference in other people's lives. I received my degree in exercise kinesiology with a minor in community health. I really wanted to be a strength and conditioning coach for professional athletes.

When I graduated with my degree, I worked as a personal trainer and also worked construction. Few things really made me happier than showing up at the gym and helping someone become better. Coaching and inspiring people have always come naturally to me.

The pay a personal trainer earned, where I was living, made it difficult to pay for the lifestyle I wanted. Over the years, I became self-conscious about being in my mid-twenties and wearing sweatpants to work (what was I thinking?). It seemed like I wasn't living in the "adult" world.

Instead of focusing on being happy and enjoying work life, I shifted my attention to my clients, who were seemingly passing me by financially. The increase in confidence my clients got from improving their physical health helped many of them grow their businesses substantially. Internally, I began to process their success as my lack of success because when I would speak to professionals I would meet away from the gym, the conversation would always turn to, "What do you do?" My answer was often met with the question, "When are you going to get a real job?" followed by laughter.

Well, over time those things began to add up, and I caved. I caved to societal pressure that dictated that I wasn't enough if I was a physical trainer. I felt I had to have a "big boy" job. So what did I do? I went into construction full time and dropped my first love of personal training and physical fitness.

Now... I don't regret my current profession of retirement planning. It allows me to help people in a significant way. However, when I left personal training, I started a decade long, often painful, journey of trying to find a place to fit in societies expectations of what I should be doing professionally. For almost a decade, it seemed that I got further and further away from my true passion and was "riding the corporate sales track".

During that time, I could always feel the pull of being a coach or trainer, but now my lifestyle was more expensive than what being a coach or trainer allowed. I too, had fallen victim (hook, line, and sinker) to what the television was telling me I needed to have at my age.

I started acquiring stuff. Professional awards and a good income had me fooled into thinking I was being true to myself. Those successes and the ability to check off life's milestones had me fooled into thinking I was on the right track. Looking back, I was being true to my ego, rather than my heart. I was feeding it with every sale I made, every award I won, and everything" I bought. However, I don't think I was really being true to my soul.

The commitment of being a husband and a father also dictated the type of income I needed to make. Like so many other people, I was caught. I was caught up in being somebody I never thought I'd be because working in my sweatpants as a fitness trainer in a gym "wasn't enough."

It's easy to see, looking back, that the person I went to school to be slowly got further and further away from me. Now, don't get me wrong. I'm not going to be closing my retirement planning practice to go back to personal training. The commitment I've made to my clients and the professional growth I've experienced are too much to give away, and I now receive a lot of fulfillment from helping clients achieve their dreams. However, when I'm able to retire from my practice and start another chapter in my life, I do not see anything standing in my way of going back and coaching people as a personal trainer or martial arts instructor, should I make that choice.

Almost all of us go through the same track/story that I just laid out. Changing tracks while we have children and commitments, during our thirties, forties, and fifties, requires a lot of courage and resources, but in retirement we have the golden opportunity to get off this track, shed the past, and really go for the life we truly want to live.

> "Money provides opportunity."
> ~ Matthew Jackson

Money

There is no doubt that the amount of financial abundance in our lives directly correlates to the amount, and type, of opportunities we enjoy. For example, if you're one of Sam Walton's children, you have many options available to you in how you choose to live your life.

Money plays an important role in our ability to live a life true to ourselves. Chances are that you have accumulated enough money in your life, or are on track to do so. Money is the key to giving yourself permission to live a life true to your dreams.

If you don't feel comfortable that your money will outlast you in retirement, go get help right now! Visit www.TheRetirementDreammaker.com to find help or to guide you in the direction that will help you best. Not having enough money will deny you the permission you need to shed the past and reshape your life.

Too many good people are intimidated about finances and investing. Rather than learn the basics and developing a better understanding of finances, many good people choose to do nothing. They say they don't trust "the system,"; they can't find a trustworthy person to help them; and that the economy and investing are constantly changing. These beliefs turn good people off.

Don't let this be you! It hurts me to talk to people so disengaged from their finances that they have no idea where they actually stand, financially, in retirement. Unfortunately, this mentality is much more common than you think. Doing some basic income and asset planning is essential in getting a clear picture of what is possible and what is not possible in retirement. Don't delay. Do this now if you have not already! Visit www.TheRetirementDreammaker.com for help.

> "No one saves us but ourselves. No one can and no one may.
> We ourselves must walk the path."
> ~ Buddha

Daily Habits

We are creatures of habit, and nothing is harder than breaking old habits. We spend a lifetime creating, developing, learning, and improving daily habits. They are the fabric that defines us.

From the time we wake up, our bathing routine, what we eat in the morning, the route we take to work, our exercise plan, the time we have at dinner, and the time we go to sleep, form the daily habits we are constantly perfecting. They are essential to success when we are growing and maintaining our family, work, and fun. Our daily habits help to keep our lives in "order".

We can control our daily habits by having the power to make them whatever we wish. Now is a great time to think about your daily habits. Are they the product of your conscious choice? Are some of them dictated to you by your family, boss, or need for money? Probably both, right?

Sure, eating a great breakfast, exercising, networking, reading, practicing daily gratitude, smiling, crushing your daily goals, and drinking enough water daily are all the product of our choice. We choose to make many of these habits in our lives in order to better execute the habits that make others happy. Shall I prove it to you?

Getting up early, being home on-time for dinner, taking out the trash, and leaving the toilet seat appropriately up or down are great examples of habits we develop for our family. They are not necessarily the daily habits we strive for on our own, but to keep the harmony in the family or to be a good example, we develop these habits for the love of others. Thank goodness, love for our family keeps pushing us to be better at these. Who knows how successful those habits might be if we were on our own?

I'm sure your boss appreciated your daily habits of showing up to work on time, giving your best effort, meeting deadlines, and having a great attitude at work. Even though these habits are expected by our employers, we still have to have the daily discipline to do them. Go ahead… pat yourself on the back. These daily habits become powerful and empowering when we get recognition as a result of being consistent in positively practicing these. Being consistent with these daily habits helps us to get ahead in life!

Are you a little short on money? Well, I'm sure we've all developed some really great habits, because we need some more money. Do you buy gas at the cheapest fill station, even if that means driving a little farther to get it? I'm sure no one has ever turned off the lights when leaving a room!

If you're already practicing some of the daily habits I mentioned, you know they can have a great effect on your daily life. I'm sure many of your daily habits are so well-developed that you don't have to even think about doing a lot of them. They are just part of who you are. They're ingrained into your persona. You automatically do them.

Isn't it interesting how many of us develop daily habits to fit in with others? Is it even more interesting that many of us struggle to develop the same positive daily habits for our own benefits? It's as if many of us are so tired of mustering the daily discipline it takes to execute the habits expected of us by others that when it comes to our own life goals, we have a hard time making the effort. Do you ever find yourself feeling this way? I know I do sometimes.

When we get this way, we subconsciously develop little habits that may not be the best for us. "Unplugging" after a long day working is something we all do. The challenge is to not let the down time we need after a long day stretch into retirement. This happens to a lot of people.

Some daily habits many of us unconsciously do after a long day at work include eating poorly, watching three hours of television before bed, smoking, drinking more alcohol than we probably should, and going to bed too late. Yes…these are daily habits we develop, practice, and perfect. They provide us comfort and consistency, but they probably aren't the best habits for us.

Don't be fooled into thinking I'm preaching that we all need to be squeaky clean in our daily habits if we want to live a life true to ourselves, or that you're not good enough if you don't. Putting out the daily effort to crush our daily habits in a positive way is very difficult to do on a daily basis. It takes focus, discipline, and sacrifice. Some days we do a great job of it and other days… not so great.

The point is we all develop daily habits that affect us deeply. When we have twenty to forty years of practicing them, we are going to have a hard time rewiring, developing, and practicing new habits. Try asking a smoker of thirty years to change his smoking habit or to ask someone who watches two to three hours of television every night to turn it off. It's tough! Asking people to alter their daily habits of more than thirty days is quite the challenge.

We've spent a good deal of time together talking about the habits we may form during our working years and while growing a family. I've had many clients share with me, over the years, how they've unwillingly outgrown many of their positive daily habits, and they are not quite sure how to reshape new habits in retirement. So, what happens when the daily habits associated with raising a family are done, because the kids have moved away? Are these daily family activities and habits replaced with television watching or learning a new skill or hobby?

When you retire, hopefully with enough money, would you let down your guard and let some of the daily personal habits waiver? After all, it's nice to not have a sense of urgency to meet a deadline, be on time, and grow personally and professionally. So how do we replace them? Do we replace them? The retirees I've spent time with continually comment on how tough it is to reshape daily habits in retirement.

I'm sharing this with you so that you may be better prepared for how hard it can be to replace the daily habits that fit into your life before retirement. When you don't have the sense of urgency to change and you feel your health may always be great, tomorrow seems like a better day to get started on developing new habits for retirement. Tomorrow turns into next week and next week turns into…well…who knows? Start today. You will never be younger and healthier!

If you have tried to create a new habit recently and made it stick for more than thirty days, give yourself a pat on the back! You know how much positive energy and commitment it takes. Later, I'm going to give you specific instructions on how you give yourself the best chance of breaking those old daily habits that chain you to the past.

> "Efforts and courage are not enough
> without purpose and direction."
> ~ John F. Kennedy

Lack of Direction

I recently had an eye-opening conversation with a client, who was to retire a month after our meeting. I was truly excited for him! As we finished up the work we were doing, I said, "Holy cow, Brian. I'm so excited for you! You've made it. It looks like you have all of your ducks in a row financially. You're going to have plenty of dough to meet your income goals. Your retirement plan is rock solid. You've got to be excited to start the third chapter of your life! What are you going to do to fill your time? What kind of passions are you going after?"

He looked at me square in the eye and said, half smiling, "You know, truthfully, I want to put down some new carpet for my wife, and I want to upgrade the kitchen after all these years." Then he trailed off and started looking around my office. I was sitting there thinking, "OK. This is the typical stuff I hear, but I'm waiting to hear about the exciting stuff. The stuff that gets HIS engine going."

So I say, "But what about after that? What are you going to do?" He turned his eyes hesitantly back at me and said, "I honestly have no idea." And then he let out a "humph." I said, "Brian, you haven't thought about something to do that you haven't been able to because of work and saving for retirement? I mean, look, you've made it! What have you been dreaming about doing?"

I'll never forget his reply. He's said to me, with an almost-discouraged expression and a half-smile, "You know...I never thought this day would come. It's been so long anyone has asked me what *I* want. I've never really given it any thought. Gosh," he said, shrugging his shoulders. "I don't know. I don't even know how to go about it finding something that interests me."

Internally, my jaw was on the floor! I couldn't believe what I was hearing. I tried to help him and put out some ideas, "Well, Brian, what did you always think about being when you were a teenager? Did you ever want to be an artist or learn to play music? Did you ever want to build a motorcycle? What about coaching a little league team? Did you ever want to do that? You should think about what you wanted to do as a kid and start there." Brian said, almost deflated, but a little encouraged, "You know, I guess I need to think about it. That might be a good place to start, but who knows?"

Lacking direction in retirement is really common. If you are near retirement, I encourage you to start thinking about what makes you tick. What would you like to do if time, money, and skills were no obstacle? If you are in retirement and can connect to Brian's story, let me help you.

Visit www.TheRetirementDreammaker.com. We have some useful tools to help provide you with some direction on to find what interests you and how to pursue that interest.

> "Happiness is not something you postpone for the future;
> it is something you design for the present."
> ~ Jim Rohn

Apathy

I believe that apathy is one of the biggest obstacles we need to break through in retirement. Most of the people whom I have worked with have no sense of urgency and have become very apathetic in retirement because they believe time is on their side and that their health will not have any impact on what they can do in retirement. They also don't consider how other peoples' health, be it spouse, child, brother or sister, will have any effect on how they live their life in retirement or follow their passion. So, people become very apathetic regarding finding urgency to go out there and pursue their dreams.

Once they become apathetic, finding a sense of urgency becomes very hard because we all believe that bad things only happen to other people. Bad health happens to other people, not us. Financial loss happens to other people, not us. Loss of time and opportunity happens to other people, not us.

The truth is that all of these things happen to us. It's inevitable. Do you know anyone whose health has improved past age 65? I don't. Do you know anyone who has needed a joint replacement after age 60? I do. Do you know anyone who died unexpectedly just before retirement or just after retirement started? I know of plenty.

So, it's really important to break the apathy mold other people fall into in retirement. Tomorrow always comes, but the opportunities of today only last today, and as the old adage goes, "don't put off until tomorrow what you can do today."

It's my belief that apathy grows and becomes stronger when we don't have the courage to face our own morbidity and mortality. We don't talk enough about having the courage to overcome apathy. It does take courage to "set our wheels in motion."

> "He who is not courageous enough to take risks will accomplish nothing in life."
> ~ Muhammad Ali

Courage

This is a topic that, flat out, does not get enough attention. I get frustrated when I read books about how to "level up" my life, personally and professionally, and not one word is mentioned about courage. It seems there is a competition among authors and speakers to see who can pump you up the most.

Who can jump around the stage with the most excitement? Who can yell the loudest? Who can be the most enthusiastic? Who can challenge the audience the most? Who can belittle the audience in the most diplomatic way, without offending anyone? Which author can stoke the fires of willpower most brightly? Who has the best smile and speaking skills that raise the audience's energy into a crashing crescendo of "Lets storm the castle! Who's with me?".

Don't get me wrong. I benefit from others' excitement, encouragement, and motivation. It's undeniable, and I truly benefit from good speakers and authors! I'm grateful to and for them. I spend a lot of my hard-earned money and valuable time learning from and being motivated by people I admire. But, let me ask you a question.

Have you ever run into someone who seemingly goes to see motivational speaker after motivational speaker and/or reads motivational book after book and never does a damn thing with their life? Oh yeah? Me too.

I don't think the people we know and meet are like this because they lack willpower or motivation. We all have the willpower to change. That's why you're reading this book. Many people have the desire to change, improve their lives, and take on new challenges, but a lot of people don't have the courage to do it.

Changing course in your life, working in the direction of your passions, and doing what is important to you takes guts and courage. This is especially true if it's different than what your family or society expects of you, and if it is different than what you normally do.

How does the retired engineer tell his spouse he wants to skydive at 68? **Courage.**
How does the widower, who finds himself alone after forty years, make connections with others? **Courage.**
How does the divorcée who has never understood finances learn better ways to structure her retirement? **Courage.**
How does the 80-year-old woman, who's been taking care of children and grandchildren all of her life, take up basketball? **Courage.**
How does the retired teacher start a business selling pastries? **Courage.**

The importance of courage in our lives is underrated. When the motivational speaker is gone, and the book of encouragement is closed, what are we left with? We are left with the courage to take action. Either we have the courage take action, or we don't. It's that simple. Action takes **courage**!

I can think of countless times in my life that I let a lack of courage get the best of me. Here's what's funny. I've hardly ever lacked courage to put my life on the line trying ridiculously dangerous skills in gymnastics. I've never lacked the courage to bow hunt in the wilds of the mountains of Colorado, in September, with only a bow and arrow, miles away from the nearest rode with no cellphone connection and my life strapped to my back in my backpack. I've never lacked the courage to rappel off of two-hundred-foot cliffs as a twenty-something-year-old. Courage has never been an obstacle of mine when grappling against much bigger and more skilled Brazilian Jiu Jitsu practitioners. It's never been a problem for me. But...

But, can you guess where a lack of courage gets the best of me sometimes? I'm sure you've experienced this too. I've lacked the courage to be true to myself in the face of judgment by other people. I'll admit it. Many times I've chickened out of pursuing things that have interested me, or telling people how I feel about them, or showing people my true self in fear of what or how my family and others are going to react. I'm sure you've experienced the same thing. Lacking courage in the face of judgment by others is very real AND very powerful.

I believe that great speakers and authors not only inspire, but they can instill courage in their audience. It takes a lot to, as I like to say, bite down on your mouthpiece, tuck your chin, and really go after what you want in life. People are going to ridicule you for living a life true to yourself. People are going to judge you because you don't fit within their box of expectations of you. Situations are going to arise that will make you doubt that if the pursuit of your passions are worth it.

I believe life is about having the courage to show up everyday. Even when you don't want to. Even when the weather is bad. Even when people are giving you a hard time. Even when life isn't cooperating. Even if you're tired. Having the courage to show up everyday and take one more step closer toward pursuing what challenges you, gives you fire, and finds you excitement in retirement is a big advantage.

Your Personal Strategy Session

Should you choose to take action in the direction of chasing your passions, you're going to find that pursuing your passion in your retirement is going to take a lot of courage. Here's the good thing: with every obstacle you encounter and conquer, your courage grows. Your confidence grows. Your success grows. It's an empowering positive cycle. I encourage you to make sure you always take a fistful of courage with you when setting out to take action in your retirement life. You're gonna need it.

CHAPTER 11
WHAT'S AVAILABLE TO YOU

> "The future belongs to those who believe
> in the beauty of their dreams."
> ~ Eleanor Roosevelt

Thankfully, we are living during a time that we are literally writing the definition of what retirement means. No generation in the history of our world has the opportunities that baby boomers are enjoying. The baby-boomer generation is the wealthiest and healthiest retiree generation in human history.

In the United States alone, it is estimated that baby boomers control approximately 70 percent of all disposable income, and, according to some reports, are set to inherit about $15 trillion dollars over the next twenty years.

Advancements in medical technology are helping baby boomers live longer and healthier lives. Modern medicine has found ways to help us live with medical conditions that used to severely limit or even kill us. Click on the television in the evening. The pharmaceutical industry spends more and more money on advertising each year. I challenge you to watch ten minutes of mainstream television without seeing a pharmaceutical advertisement.

The positive consequences are that we can expect to live much longer and healthier in retirement, AND baby boomers have the financial resources to handle it. For the first time in history, many of our boomers are faced with living twenty or more years in retirement. Furthermore, their ability to physically travel and digitally connect with others has never been better either.

With all of these advantages, I still hear baby boomers commenting on their concerns about what to do with their time and money during retirement. Believe it or not, not many people are talking about how to recreate life in retirement and the challenges they'll experience trying to do so.

I believe that when you have your finances secured and your income guaranteed, you have the power to be the pioneers of your lives in retirement. So, what is available to you? Anything you can imagine for yourself. Now is the time to live the life you've imagined, in your mind's eye. It's going to take some introspection, but it is available to you! I'll prove it to you!

CHAPTER 12
THE TRIANGLE OF SUCCESS

Contrary to popular belief, as a pre-retiree or retiree I feel you are at the pinnacle of your life. The media and the corporate world want you to believe you have no more value; you lack connection to technology; you don't have the energy to keep up; and you have no ability to learn new skills. Well, I think the naysayers are dead wrong!

As a pre-retiree or retiree you are at the ultimate level in what I call the "Triangle of Success".

THE TRIANGLE OF SUCCESS

Personal/Professional Life Skills

FULFILLMENT

Money   **Time**

Hopefully, over the last number of decades you've been, in some way, shape, or form, improving your skills. You know you have. While you may feel you still have room for improvement, you should be at the best time in your life when your skills are sharpened and honed. The experience and wisdom you've gained over the years can help you avoid future pitfalls, streamline your road to success in the future, and give you the confidence to pursue the third chapter in your life with optimism, energy, and success.

It does not matter what your career path was in the past. The fact is you have a significant advantage starting the third chapter of life, compared to when you started your second chapter of life (working), with very little skills, almost no experience, and very little money.

Whether you've been a high-powered corporate professional or a homemaker, you have a skill set, and that skill set is your base going forward. Don't minimize your skills and experience if you feel like other people are more skilled than you. It's not about measuring yourself next to others. This is about you, your skills, your experience and how you now are able to leverage them going forward to help you live a life true to yourself.

Too often, I work with people who don't give themselves credit for being at the top of their game. I constantly run into baby boomers who suffer from the fear of being inadequate. They are filled with low self-confidence and a sense of uncertainty. Well, I've got news for you! Any obstacles you may have had in the past that prevented you from living a life true to yourself are just an illusion. You are good enough! You have the skills you need to live a life true to yourself!

You have not worked twenty to forty years just to call it quits in the game of life. This is not the time to roll over and coast! There is no need to be anyone other than the person you want to be and to live the life you really want. Now is the time to be and do whatever it is that you've delayed for years. It doesn't matter if lack of time, money, or personal/professional skills held you back in the past.

Now is your time to put all of these attributes together and let them work for you. The excuses of needing to accumulate more money or create more time in your schedule in order to find fulfillment are over. All of the permissions you have been waiting for have been given to you. You have the green light!

You are at a time in your life when you have the most money to support your highest skillsets and an ocean of time in front of you to pursue what you've put off for years while working and being responsible for your family.

Too many retirees report, after a few years of being retired, the frustrations of boredom, lack of purpose, depression, and isolation. Retirement is an expectation you live up to. If you're feeling retirement is purposeless or that you are no longer valuable, have nothing to contribute, and can't restart your passion, I've got news for you. That's exactly what retirement will be for you.

Lack of purpose can be linked to depression. Depression is linked to lower-functioning immune systems. Lower-functioning immune systems are linked to sickness. Sickness is linked to isolation. Isolation leads to depression, and now the cycle repeats itself.

This is not the retirement lifestyle waiting for you!

Science has shown that professors working in their nineties have the same number of brain neurons as professors working in their thirties. It's all connected to the brain and how you think.

Purpose-driven lives have hope. Hope creates excitement. Excitement creates positive effects in the body, like an increase in immune function.

So what's the alternative reality of retirement to the retirement expectation described above? It's whatever you make it!

I believe that your retirement will be a period in your life of great fulfillment.

Anything and everything is available to you in retirement. You just have to have the correct mindset.

You have the ability and permission to wake up everyday fired up to make a positive change in your life. Don't act "your age," and don't limit what you can do based on what others' expect of you at your age. Each day you now have the unique opportunity to grow physically, emotionally, and spiritually without the obstacles of time, skill, and money. The triangle of success is supporting you and should be used for the benefit of growing your comfort zone, improving daily, and making a big difference in your world.

Your Personal Strategy Session

What *is* waiting for you is a new chapter of growth in your life, and it doesn't matter what your background is, how much money you have in the bank, how big your circle of influence is, how able you are to travel, or what your ability is to connect through the internet.

The third chapter of growth in your life is unique and individual to every one of us. You have the unique opportunity to expand and grow individually and have a passionate life, each new day. You have the power to pursue anything that interests you, drives you, and fills your soul with passion and excitement in retirement. You have a great ability to make positive changes in your lifestyle, and, if you choose, those who surround you.

What is waiting for you is a life of happiness, excitement, value, contribution, and fulfillment!

CHAPTER 13

3 TOOLS TO USE TO YOUR ADVANTAGE

> "The only way to predict the future is to
> have the power to shape the future."
> ~ Eric Hoffer

We have some very powerful tools to help us shape the future we want for ourselves. These 3 simple tools can powerfully launch our lives higher!

Access to Information

We have the ability to access any topic we are interested in more than any other time period in history. The days of going to the library to research your favorite subjects in books is long gone. The tedious and long task of pouring through magazine after magazine to find information on a specific topic is all but dead.

From the comfort of your own home, you have the ability access information anywhere on the globe through the internet, quickly and efficiently.

Simply click on your favorite search engine of your Internet browser, type in whatever question you have or topic you're interested in, and "POW", you have pages of results of information.

Our ability to get free education at home or anywhere in the world is available to us instantly. Do you want to learn how to bake for the first time? Search YouTube. Do you want to learn about meditation? There are hundreds of instructional videos available for free on the internet. Do you want to explore starting a local charity and getting the word out to help others? You can find out how to do it and find others who have done it simply by conducting a search on your computer!

> The internet erases the excuse of not knowing how to increase your level of understanding on any topic you are passionate about because you are geographically isolated, physically challenged, or lack money and access to information and people like-minded with you.

Information about anything your passionate about is waiting for you. You just have to have the ability to create the curiosity and excitement to explore your own mind. If you can see it and believe it, you can achieve it.

Ease of Travel

Our ability to travel safely and easily to any destination is available to all retirees. The networks of transportation are endless. We can get to literally almost anywhere we can imagine traveling by plane, train, boat, automobile, or bike.

Isolation from people and places is no longer a barrier with our freedom to move safely around the world. What is often a barrier to our ability to travel is our own insecurity. Our fears of the unknown, different people, lifestyles, food, currency, and tradition keep many peoples' feet stuck right where there are.

If you can muster the strength to overcome those insecurities and expand your comfort zone, the world is your playground. I talk to many retirees who are hesitant to travel to different places in the United States because the unknown intimidates them. Remember the talk we had about courage earlier?

They are worried about tourist traps, dishonest people, or the unknown expenses associated with travelling. What these people and everyone can really expect to encounter are others who have the same mindset. In almost any place, there are people who are willing to exchange their views, offer their experiences, and share their time.

I like travelling with a purpose. To me, travelling to meet people from other places who have the same interests as I do is fun and fulfilling. I believe travelling for retirees can be a lot less intimidating and much more exciting if you can find an event or conference that will be attracting people who have the same interests as you.

I really enjoy travelling for work to share ideas with people from other parts of the country and globe because I learn how people in my professional area of interest are handling the same challenges I face. It helps me to better serve my clients.

As a retiree, you have the same resources available to you without involving the work aspect. You can transfer the benefits of traveling for work to traveling for your passion simply and easily.

Often, when I travel for work, I am able to find a place that teaches and trains one of my passions, Brazilian Jiu Jitsu. If I don't know anyone in a place I am traveling to, I know I can easily find like-minded people by getting in a great class or training session with others who like to train like I do. It completely takes away the anxiety of being isolated no matter where I travel. I always leave training with a fresh perspective on new techniques and a fun window into the mindsets of the local people.

You can have the same experience by finding people who have the same interests as you when you travel. For example, let's say you've had a dream about visiting San Francisco and want an authentic experience instead of diving into the typical touristy types of activities. If you love to cook, for example, find a local business that offers the type of cooking classes you're interested in. The possibilities of finding new friends in new places are endless. Use your travel to expand and grow your passion in anything from exercise, meditation, cooking, personal growth, car shows, fishing, writing, painting, and so on.

Take a chance, and do some research on your travel destination to get connected to local people who have the same interests as you. You'll share ideas and gain fresh perspectives. All of the times I get out of my comfort zone to do this, I grow my understanding of other people, and the connection we all have. My gratitude for my individual life grows as well.

Connection Any Way You Can Imagine It

So how do we create connection in retirement? That can be a tough question for a lot of people to answer.

I've worked with so many people who feel isolated after a short time in retirement. Think about it. We spend so much time being a part of a group, company, or a tribe of like-minded people through decades at work, and then one day we're expected to leave and replace a major part of our day, identity, and essence with...? For most retirees, the answer is.... uhhhh... I'm not really sure.

When was the last time a representative from the Human Resources department said, "Hey, congratulations, you're retiring! Let us help you understand the challenges you face socially and help you create a new identity in retirement because this part of your life is over." It just doesn't happen. They are most likely happy to get you out of the door and say good riddance.

So, you should expect to find opportunities to create connections in any way you can imagine. You are fully able to attract, seek, and create opportunities to engage with people who have the same interests as you from around the globe.

One of my hobbies is archery. Although there is a great archery club in my home town, I am just flat out too busy to attend the shoots and meetings at the times they have them. However, I was able to re-create the connection with other archers in another way.

Years ago, I found a forum of archers interested in the same style of archery I am. It's awesome because I can stay connected to the pulse of my hobby, on my time, and in the way I want to.

If I want to read a forum board and learn about a particular subject of archery I am interested in, I don't have to work my schedule around a 7 p.m. meeting. I can pull up the forum at 5:15 a.m., while having coffee. At 9:30 p.m., rather than watching TV, I go to the forum to find all the latest tips on what I am interested in.

To take it one step further, if I need a question answered or have information to contribute from my experiences, I can simply post on the forum board and wait for interaction from other forum members throughout the day or on the following days.

Let's expand that reality one step further. A couple of times a year there are archery meet-ups. At those meet-ups you can camp, shoot, cook, swap stories, share ideas and create friendships. The cool thing is, if I choose, I can travel to a destination, see new scenery, meet new people, and contribute my knowledge to something I care about, all while hanging out with other cool like-minded people. I don't have to if I don't want to, and if I don't have the time to show up in person, I can still interact with my "tribe" of people whenever it's convenient for me.

I'll admit, when I first started searching for like-minded people, the internet wasn't as full of groups like the ones I have found, but you should explore what's possible now. There is literally a whole universe of possibilities at your very fingertips.

The hardest part is stepping into the threshold of connection to see what happens. There's that courage thing again. If you find and try a community, and you don't like the people, attitudes, or opinions you see, you can simply close your browser and move on. No awkward good-byes or we'll miss yous. Then go search for another community.

The internet gives us all equal opportunity to create connection, no matter our financial achievements, locality, language, race, or gender. Have you ever felt like a floating island in an ocean? Have you ever had a particular interest or lacked meaningful conversation about a subject you're interested in and don't have people locally to interact with?

Expand your comfort zone! Do a digital search for groups in your area with the same interests. You may surprise yourself and find people within a short driving distance you can meet face-to-face, or you may be able to interact with someone halfway across the country that may give you tips on how to grow and share your passions.

The point is that connection is waiting for you. Never risk letting your passions die because you don't have like-minded people in your area or don't care for the communities around you. You can grow and develop your passions by simply shifting your thinking more digitally.

The benefit for you is the ignition of the flame and the fueling of your passion. We all need fuel to add to our passion fires. Connection provides that for us. Don't wait. Don't make excuses. Go find your tribe. Be a part of it. Contribute. Receive. Grow. Make the world a better place with your own expertise and interests. That's a big step toward having a fulfilling retirement!

Contribution to your passion by passing on your knowledge and experience creates fulfillment. The media has it all wrong. As a retiree, you have invaluable worth and can make contributions in ways that really matter to you.

> "A man is not old until regrets take the place of dreams."
> ~ John Barrymore

The New You is waiting for you! For some of you, this may be the first time in your life you are 100 percent fully in charge of your future. That's scary as hell to of a lot of people. For the first time, no one is dictating what time you need to wake up, where you have to go, what you need to wear, whom you have to call, and when you are able to travel.

You are 100 percent responsible for the consequences for your choices. Top to bottom. From the beginning of your day to the end. You are not alone if you feel frozen. You are not alone if you ask yourself, "Well, where the heck do I start?"

The old construct of retirement is dead. Fulfillment does not die at retirement. Waiting for life to happen to you is no way to live out the third chapter of your life. I tell my clients to start with what's most important to them. Instead of focusing on creating worth through the acceptance of others, the key is to create new self-worth by rewriting the new you and what defines you.

We inherently define our success and fulfillment based upon the achievements of our children and the highlights of our careers, but what if that family is successfully independent of you, and your career is over? How is it possible to create the new definition of success and fulfillment?

FOLLOWING YOUR PASSIONS

 You're never too old to follow a passion.

 You will encounter adversity on the road to following your passion. The adversity will come in all shapes and sizes, whether it's an injury, or friends saying you're crazy for following a passion. No matter what, it will lead to personal growth.

 Happiness leads to a healthy life.

 Community can create happiness, and we all need some sort of community. It doesn't matter if your community is the homeless or a basketball team.

Simply redefine the old construct. Rather than associating your success with the success of your family or what you have achieved in your career, try associating your success with being the very best you.

I had a shift in my life when I was able to do that. I used to find value in my importance to others, but I would always find myself frustrated when I gave my best effort with the best intentions, and it wasn't received the way I hoped.

For example, I would feel rejected, let down, and unappreciated if a person I helped wouldn't acknowledge my efforts with a quick response of praise or appreciation. I found myself frustrated in my passions and work, giving my best effort, but not getting the same in return.

Nowadays, acknowledgements from my family or in my career no longer dictate my fulfillment. I now focus on being the best I can be every day, surrounding myself with love, and expanding my comfort zones. I've been able to stamp out boredom, frustration, and lack of excitement by not tying my fulfillment to how others might react.

I now find much more fulfillment in knowing that in every interaction I have with family, at work and/or pursuing my passions, I am giving my best effort, surrounding myself with loving supportive people, and expanding my comfort zones. If I can check yes to each of those pillars every day, I can go to sleep excited for tomorrow, no matter how anyone reacted to me.

I no longer let life happen to me based on others' reactions. Life is now happening through me, based upon my effort and what is important to me. It is available to you also. Shake up your life! I want you to hack your retirement based upon what is important to you, rather than fitting in the mold of what others tell you how you should be living your retirement. That's nonsense!

When you don't define your fulfillment by the reactions around you or your physical abilities, you open yourself up to being able to rewrite your own story, as you change and others change around you.

Take for example, Morrie Boogart, a 91-year-old Grandville, Michigan man who knitted hats for the homeless from his hospice bed. He's made over 8,000 caps for the homeless.

"I do it awfully slow; it maybe takes me two days to make a hat."

He spends his days in hospice care at Cambridge Manor in Grandville, slowly wrapping yarn around the pegs of the loom one by one.

"The only time I'm not doing it is if I fall asleep," confesses Boogart.

Moorie embodies the definition of hacking the new construct of retirement. Although he is in a hospice, he is not tying his happiness to his physical abilities or his personal past. Instead, he's found fulfillment through what makes him happy.

"Why do I do it? It just makes me feel good," said Boogart. "It's not so much of a story, but it means a lot to me," said Boogart.

Moorie is making life happen around him rather than having his illness happen to him.

Have you ever heard of Meg Skinner and Grace Larson? Both are ninety-one and play basketball for the San Diego Senior Women's Basketball Association on a team named The Splash. Larson told ESPNW, "I was 78 when I got my first basketball shoes, so that was a thrill."

In an article for GoodHousekeeping.com, the author Sarah Schreiber wrote, "Since it's now medically proven that seniors' social connectedness leads to longer, more fulfilling lives, it comes as no surprise that many Splash players have outlived their significant others, siblings and life-long friends." Another great quote in the story: "A lot of my childhood friends thought I was crazy at 66 to be playing basketball. They said, 'You'll break an arm, you'll break a leg,'" explained 87-year-old Marge Carl. "You know, I'm the only one surviving of my childhood friends. They're all gone, every one of them."

"You've got to get engaged," Marge told the San Diego Tribune in 2016. "You can't sit in a room watching TV. That's a death knell."

With over six million views, ESPNW's viral and moving video on the Splash is saliently titled "Splash Sisters." That's what these teammates are, plain and simple. "Friendship, a sisterhood, a family" is how Larson describes her team: "It's the nicest group of people from all walks of life." (http://www.goodhousekeeping.com/life/inspirational-stories/news/a44876/80-year-old-female-basketball-team/)

Here are a couple of gems I've learned from this story about following passions.

#1 You're never too old to follow a passion.

#2 You will encounter adversity on the road to following your passion. The adversity will come in all shapes and sizes, whether it's an injury, or friends saying you're crazy for following a passion. No matter what, it will lead to personal growth).

#3 Happiness leads to a healthy life.

#4 Community can create happiness, and we all need some sort of community. It doesn't matter if your community is the homeless or a basketball team.

> "...It's now medically proven that seniors' social connectedness leads to longer, more fulfilling lives..."
> ~ Sarah Schreiber

In Closing

Stories like this really encourage me to defy my age. They help me see what is possible in my retirement life. When reading stories like this, it's hard to imagine that Bronnie Ware's 2009 discovery could actually be true. Unfortunately, the truth is there are many more people out there who would confirm Bronnie's discovery that people regret not going after their wildest dreams than people like the ones in the stories we just read, who went for their passions in their later years.

To be fair to all of us, it's natural to deny the fact that our bodies are changing with age and that bad health, bad circumstances, and bad times don't happen to us. We all would prefer to believe they happen to other people. It's a major contributing factor to our unwillingness to take action now and to take the steps needed to follow our own passions and live a life true to our deepest desires.

Your Personal Strategy Session

To recap, there are other obstacles in the way that keep us from living a life true to ourselves. Familial expectations, societal pressures, money, our own daily habits, lack of direction, apathy, and a lack of courage to live our most authentic life can be big obstacles for true happiness and fulfillment in retirement.

The great news is that you are at the best point in time in your life to overcome those obstacles. It's likely that at no other point of time in your life have you had more money, better life skills, and more time than right now.

Your access to information, your ability to travel and your ability to create connections has never been easier at any other point in history. You have everything you need to live a life true to yourself. Your courage to make changes and take the necessary steps will be challenged but knowing that in advance can help you stay the course.

In the next chapters, we will look deeper into how to take action and how to develop new daily habits. We are going to explore ways to strengthen our relationships, and expand personal growth and development in retirement. First, I'm going to give you a simple exercise to set your wheels in motion in the direct you want to go!

HOW TO TAKE ACTION

CHAPTER 14
SETTING YOUR WHEELS IN MOTION

"When developing a new discipline, if you can do it for thirty consecutive days, you have a great likelihood of developing that new discipline into a positive daily habit."
~ Mark Goldberg

If you've been inspired to make the effort to create a new source of fulfillment in your life and have mustered the courage to take a step in that direction, you will most likely need to develop some new habits that will ensure you stay the course.

So how do we get started designing new habits?

Designing new habits takes a lot of self-evaluation and honesty. It's not an easy skill to develop, because you have to be able to look at yourself honestly, step outside of your own skin, and look at where you're at now and where you want to be at three years from now. One of the best things I believe that I can help others with is how to best design your new habits and make them stick.

It's really very easy.

Creative Visualization – Meditation - Mindfulness

Years ago, I began meditating. Now for those of you who are worried that I'm about to go off on a hippie trip, let me define what I mean by meditation. Meditation, for me, is the same as making a mental goal sheet in the morning of what I'd like to get done for the day or the week and creating a reminder of where I would like to be a few years from now.

I can't sit with my legs crossed over each other and chant "Ohm" for hours. My meditation is a version of the creative visualization and focused intention of how I want to best dictate or direct my life. Somewhere around 1983, I was first introduced to the power of creative visualization when I was competing. We had a trainer who had worked with athletes at the United States Olympic Training Center. He had been working with athletes and showing them how creative visualization could improve their athletic performance. Studies have shown that creative visualization (I'm calling it meditation/strategy sessions from now on) does improve focus, decrease stress, and improve athletic performance.

We had a very powerful exercise that would take about thirty minutes, and we could do the visualization at any time of the day or before bedtime. Here's what it looks like.

1. Clearing the mind and body of stress and anxiety through focused breathing. We would, for a few minutes, only focus on our breathing and count up to ten during inhalation and countdown to ten during exhalation. While we were doing focused breathing, we would be also concentrating on the relaxation of all of the muscles in our body.

2. We would mentally perform an individual skill we were working on with perfection and ease. Then we would incorporate that perfect skill in our routine (or set as we called them). Last, we would mentally perform each skill ten times, paying close attention to each detail.

3. We began by seeing ourselves getting prepared to perform the skill.

4. Then, touching the equipment, we would mentally take in the sights, sounds, and smells, and feeling the air around us.

5. Next, we would begin the skill focusing on the breath we would use (inhalation for exhalation).

6. We would pay close attention to what muscles were tight and triggered and which were relaxed and loose.

7. Then as we were mentally completing the skill, we would focus on the specific timing we needed to be successful, the feeling of gravity working on our bodies, where and how we would push or pull on the various equipment at the precise correct time to do what we needed to do to execute with perfection.

8. Last, we would mentally focus on what position we would end up in after the skill was perfectly completed and how that made us feel.

We would do this ten times. Then we would expand this out to incorporating the skill into an entire set in practice, and lastly, we would expand this out into the next competition we were training for. Each expansion would be a repeat of the prior. Meaning, no matter the level of expansion (singular skill, complete set in practice, or competition), we paid particular attention to every detail we could handle mentally.

We drilled down the exact physical and emotional experiences our senses of touch, sight, sound, and the emotions we would experience before, during, and after each level. All the time focusing on the desired positive outcome we wanted, which was perfect execution and doing our best to perfection.

I know this had a dramatic effect on my performance and helped me to decrease anxiety during competitions. Not only had I put in the physical time on the equipment, but before bedtime, I had a routine of lying in bed and doing more mental work, engraining the muscle patterns in my brain without even touching the equipment.

At a competition, it seemed as if I went on autopilot. There was little that was unfamiliar, so distractions of the unknown or unfamiliar were kept to a minimum. I was thereby able to increase my ability to focus without distraction. Each time I saluted the judge before each set, all I had to do was clear my mind and mentally hit the "go" button.

It was amazing how easily I would get in the flow and execute with confidence. This meditation was a simple but effective way to direct my life the way I had envisioned and to get what I wanted in competition. No matter where I ended up on the podium, my only desire was to execute to the best of my ability, as close to my perfection as possible.

In 2012 or so, I began to incorporate this mediation/strategy sessions into all areas of my life (personal, professional, relationship, physical, emotional, and spiritual) with great positive result. This has helped me to shape my life into whatever I would like it to be and whatever direction I would like it to go, and so can you. Whether that is during your working years or in retirement.

Everyday, I do an exercise reminding myself of where I came from, where I'm at now, and where I want to go. Vishen Lakhiani, co-founder of Mindvalley mentioned a statement that really resonated with me in 2016.

> "We, as humans, tend to overestimate what we can do in six months and underestimate what we can do in three years."
> ~ Vishen Lakhiani

That statement really resonates with me because in our society, especially as Americans, we want everything now; we demand life within five minutes. If we can't get it within five minutes, it's not fast enough or worth it. The problem with that attitude is that when we are designing six-month goals, we tend to think we can get all of this inspired stuff done super quick. When, in fact, while we're chasing dreams and developing passions, we have to let time pass, so they can grow.

It's no different than when we plant a garden. We plant a seed. We water it. We wait for the sunlight to warm the soil. We wait for the soil to warm. Then, we wait for the seed shell to crack and the sprout to break the surface of the soil. Finally, we wait for the sprout to grow inch by inch into a fully mature plant.

It's, also, no different for us when we are designing our own new habits. Sometimes, in our "now" culture we forget we need to water our passions. We need to fertilize our passions, and it takes time for life to create the energy that gives us the ability to fully realize our passions.

Objectivity

Real objectivity requires daily discipline, and that's the dirty little secret. Our passions don't magically spring out of us. They need our daily discipline to develop and our passions do need pruning to reach full potential.

I believe it's very important when we are designing new habits, as Vishen stated, that we keep our eyes focused on the long-term three-year goal. Being from Colorado, I like to think of it as keeping our eyes focused on the top of the mountain, as opposed focusing solely on taking the steps right in front of me.

It's one of the things I used to do when hiking in the mountains of Colorado. Often times, if I was on a backpacking trip, and we had a long hike in front of us, we would begin our hike at night or well before the pre-dawn sunlight in order to prevent me from focusing on the step-by-step-by step climb up a long route to the top of a mountain.

That way, in my mind's eye, I could envision the peak that I would want to get to and the long-term result, instead of hiking it during the day, having to look at the constant pitch in front of me and the rocks I would have to crawl over and deal with. The mental challenge of having a mountain to face, step after step, while carrying a heavy backpack and constantly looking up, would steal the resolve of even the toughest adventurer. It's no different when reshaping your own personal habits to reshape your life.

When you design your new habits, I think it's really important to objectively evaluate where you are now, where you want to be in six months, and where you want to be three years from now. One of the best ways you can get yourself on the right path, so you know the new habits you need to develop to get you to reach your maximum fulfillment is by taking Janet Attwood's "Passion Test."

Discover Your Passions

You can simply visit her by going to www.ThePassionTest.com. Janet has written a beautiful exercise that I've benefited from that can also help you. If you are uncertain of the direction that your passion lays or what your strongest passion is, you can't possibly know the course that you have to take to get you there.

I encourage you to do the exercise to help guide you to where you ultimately want to be three years from now in order to get the most fulfillment out of the third chapter of your life. Don't delay!

By completing The Passion Test, you may quickly find out what interests you most, and from there, you'll shape how you want to develop your new daily discipline. This will help you set out on the right path to get you to where you want to be.

CHAPTER 15
GET SOME TRACTION

> "Words without action are like wheels without traction.
> It is how you live that counts."
> ~ Geoff Thompson

How do you redesign the new schedule of your life and make it stick?

I'm a firm believer that daily discipline helps us to overcome the daily distractions that prevent us from following our true passions. What are the distractions I'm talking about?

They are the distractions of family and friends telling you that your passions are unrealistic, and that you need to stay within their comfort zone (their definition of you and how they see you). The distractions of people asking you for your time because they believe you have plenty to give without having a job to go to every day. I'm talking about the distractions of your own self-doubts and your former habits.

Without the daily discipline of staying focused on where you want to take your passions and how you want to live a passionate life in retirement, those distractions will ultimately stop you flat in your footsteps and prevent you from getting the most out of your retirement. The reason why I'm sharing this with you is because I want you to be fully aware that completing the passion test does not mean you are going to automatically or successfully move your life in a new direction.

Identifying and Avoiding Adversity and Distractions

If you know and can identify the challenges that you are going to face in reshaping the old construct of retirement you will be better able to overcome them and ultimately be successful in living a passionate, fulfilling retirement. Just know that you will meet some of the same adversity following your passions in retirement that you had while working. The good thing is that overcoming those challenges creates confidence in retirement, and confidence leads to success. It's a positive upward spiral.

So by knowing and identifying some of these distractions you will be better able to walk right past them. Here's an example.

My family traveled to Thailand in 2017 on a family adventure. One of the things that we did before we came here was to research the top ten scams that you could experience while adventuring throughout Thailand.

One that we came across was two people working together. They would have a spotter looking for "tourists." When that person spotted you, he or she would try to lead you to an off entrance of a landmark or tourist attraction that you were walking to see.

If the spotter was able to distract you from the main entrance and lead you to an off- entrance, you will be met by the second person in the scam. This person would politely tell you the attraction or landmark is closed, but for a price, they can get you in. All along the place is open, but they would try to get you to pay an unnecessary fee to enter.

We would have fallen for this scam, hook, line, and sinker, if it weren't for my brilliant wife. I had forgotten all about the scam, but thankfully my wife hadn't. As we left the Temple of The Dawn in Bangkok and rode a water taxi across the river to walk through the Grand Palace of Thailand, I wasn't paying attention to my surroundings.

This fella with a really big smile approached me and said, "Are you from the U.S.? Do you speak English? Are you wanting to see the Grand Palace?" Instead of saying, "Mai Ben Rai," (meaning I'm OK), I said, "yes".

He looked at all three of us as we were walking and said, "Oh, you can go right through here." As I looked away from the line of people we were walking with, there was a nice, quiet side entrance in the twenty-five foot wall. Little did I know, as I stood in awe of the enormity of the Palace, that it was a side service entrance. Duh!

Without even thinking I crossed the street where he was directing us with my daughter and wife in tow. As we approached the entrance, his partner, who was casually leaning up against the wall, met us, and said, with a smile, "I'm sorry, friends, the Palace is closed today, but I'll let you in for $15 per person. My wife walked right past him and said "Nope, we're going in," and that's when a palace guard, inside the wall, saw us and said "excuse me, you cannot enter through here."

My wife and I instantly looked at each other and smiled, turned around to laugh at the second accomplice, but in an instant, he was gone and blended into the crowd. Ha! Thank goodness my wife recognized the scam and walked past, because I was about to pull out my wallet and pay, determined to see the amazing Grand Palace.

The point of this story is that it's important to know the distractions you face as you reshape your life. If you can't identify these distractions, you're going to fall for them. I want you to know that you will come up against these challenges in the third chapter of your life that will distract you from pursuing your passion and fulfillment.

Having the daily discipline of staying focused on what you really want in the third chapter of your life, three years from now, is really important. So how do we develop those daily disciplines?

In my personal life, I have a simple system that I use to help me stay on track toward my three-year goals of being the best I can be. Here's what I do.

Winning The Day Before It Even Starts

Each morning, when I get up with my cup of espresso, I clear my head and shake off the night's sleep, and I get started on my meditation/strategy session for the day. Each morning, for twenty to thirty minutes, I focus on being grateful for yesterday and where I want to be three years from now. I then meditate on where I'm at, whom I'm with, what I'm doing, and how it feels and sounds, and what it smells and looks like.

Then I focus on what I have to do that particular day to get me closer to where I want to be three years from today. I envision my perfect day. I envision waking up and having a wonderful morning experience with my family. I envision how I feel energized after my short workout. I envision how good my shower is going to feel. I envision my perfect day at work. I envision helping clients and prospective clients with ease and fun. I envision my perfect drive home from work and last, I envision myself doing whatever it is I want to do after work on that particular day. It could be working on a project at home, washing my car, going to train martial arts, enjoying dinner with my wife, and watching my daughter at her practice.

I try to bring in the feeling of gratitude, happiness, confidence, and love as I envision each of these events happening throughout the day.

After I'm done with my daily meditation/strategy session, I do my quick daily exercises. I find that if I don't do my simple exercise routine in the morning, I get too distracted from the day and don't get it done. I try to train in martial arts three to five times per week, but sometimes duty calls at work, and I can't make a lunch workout. But I can still have the satisfaction of getting some physical activity in by getting my short routine done.

Here's what I do. You can modify something like this in your life. After my morning strategy session, I immediately do my fifty push-ups to keep my upper body in shape. Then I immediately hold a plank position (only toes and forearms touching the ground) for ninety seconds, followed by ten to thirty more push-ups, depending on how I'm feeling from the previous day's workout.

When I first started this routine, I struggled with twenty-two push-ups and forty-five-second planks. If you're not the physical exercise type of person, no worries, this is just my routine. Let's not judge what we can or can't do.

After I complete my morning strategy session and a quick workout, I grab a quick breakfast and read for five to ten minutes of whatever I want to read, and then I head to the shower. Now here's my secret sauce to creating confidence in myself, which I believe leads to my success.

On my bathroom mirror, written in dry erase marker are words or phrases of encouragement. At the time of writing these words, I have written on my mirror, "I am one step closer to being the best I can possibly be!" I know that I need that daily reminder of my past success of yesterday and the encouragement to go after what I want today. This daily reminder helps me to act in the direction that I want to take my life, rather than react to how life is acting on me.

Under the word or phrase of encouragement, I have an accountability record. It's really simple, but it's super powerful for me. I have written the underlined words daily strategy session, push-ups, reading. Each day I complete each of these I put a tick mark under the appropriate word.

Now don't be fooled and think that I do these every single day. I'm human just like you, and sometimes I have a late night, or feel really tired from a mentally exhausting day at work or physically tired because of a hard training day on the mat and just don't get my routine done. The accountability record helps me to refocus on the days I'm feeling absolutely mentally or physically drained in the morning to get back to my routine.

I'm amazed by the feeling of satisfaction I get from tallying the tick marks every month. I love looking at how many tick marks actually show up under each of these categories. This is my secret sauce for success! The days that I feel drained and do my morning strategy sessions without doing my workout immediately after, or I do my meditation and workout, but don't do my reading, I'm quietly reminded when I look at myself in the mirror and know that I have to tally my action.

It's so funny how these accountability words can inspire me and keep me honest and on track with my daily discipline. I can't tell you how many times I've read my action phrase and tallied off my daily strategy session tick mark, then looked at push-ups knowing I can't make a tick mark. It's not long before I slowly drop to floor to start my push-ups.

It's so powerful to hold yourself accountable when the reminder is staring directly at you in the mirror. So the days I find it hard to stay dedicated to my daily discipline, I don't need a spouse, friend, or drill sergeant to refocus me. I have the reminder and the encouragement staring plainly at my face.

This is why I mentioned earlier that developing new habits requires daily self-evaluation and honesty. You will be rewarded for your honest self-evaluation by the daily affirmations of making tally marks as you work to follow your passions by developing daily habits.

I believe that when I can rule the morning, it is easier for me to avoid the daily distractions that work against me. When I can clear my mind and stay focused on what I want to get done on that particular day, it's much easier for me to be successful.

After I've showered, I write down my daily goal list on paper. I do this so that I can check them off one by one throughout the day and mentally build a sense of daily accomplishment and fulfillment. These goals change daily.

These are the daily steps that help me to avoid daily distractions and fulfill my passion of being the best I can be physically, emotionally, and spiritually better in my ultimate goals three years from now.

I'm sharing this with you because many retirees I speak with have a really hard time getting started developing new daily disciplines because of the lack of urgency, direction, and passion in their lives. Too many seniors share with me that when the retirement honeymoon is over, they are left wondering "what's next." They have lost the urgency and daily discipline to direct the action in their lives, and they find themselves reacting to life.

I would encourage you, after you have taken The Passion Test and have discovered where you really want to be doing in three years, to write it down somewhere where you can see it everyday. It doesn't matter if it's written on your bathroom mirror, held on your refrigerator with a magnet, or taped as in image on the window where you do dishes, or kept in a journal. I would encourage you to put it where you can see it everyday. Just like when you were working, I also encourage you to keep a daily goal list and write down the top three things you want to accomplish that particular day.

Small Daily Goals Can Lead To Big Accomplishments

I keep my daily goal list separate from everything else, so that I can use it as a daily reference. Each day I read yesterday's goal list to make sure I accomplished what I intended too. If I didn't get all of my goals completed for the previous day, they go-to the top of what I need to do today. Each

Monday, I simply scan each daily goal sheet to see if there were any goals without checkmarks of completion next to them, so that I can make sure I don't forget to get them done this week.

Your Personal Strategy Session

It's a fun and excellent exercise that helps me to stay focused on taking the necessary steps to doing the best I can to get the most fulfillment out of my life. Yes, sometimes, daily goals do fall through the cracks, but this system helps me to never lose sight of them. The side benefit of these daily discipline action lists is that it seems to take the work out of our of work and make it more fun. When you're following your passions and carrying a responsibility of improving yourself and your life, lacking fun can really kill your motivation. Having a daily record and reviewing your accomplishments creates that fun and builds positive energy in your life.

CHAPTER 16
SMOKING THE TIRES

"Every human being is the author of his own health or disease."
~ Buddha

The Power Of Showing Up

I've structured my life with passions to help me grow physically, emotionally, and spiritually. If you are inspired to continually grow throughout your life in the same way, here's an example of how my passions help me grow in these directions.

The passion that helps my physical growth is Brazilian Jiu Jitsu. The passion that helps me grow emotionally is meditation/strategy sessions and learning about personal growth. The passion that helps me grow spiritually is reading and reflecting. Each day, I'm expanding my comfort zone with these three passions.

Life is tough, and I'll be honest. There are days I don't feel like doing any of these. Other areas of my life want to distract me and pull me away from my passions. There are days, I don't want to bump fists, slap hands, and simulate murder with my friends on the mat at Brazilian Jiu Jitsu. I'm just flat out tired or feeling insecure about my abilities. There are days I feel like I have a lot to do, and I don't want to slow down to meditate. There are days when I've been reading all day and don't want to read or practice spirituality.

It's those days that it's most important to show up. You're going to have these days too. You'll have that little voice in the back of your head saying, "What are you doing? You're retired; you should be taking it easy. You can't make a difference. You're too old. Act your age." You will hear these words. I guarantee it.

It's on these days, if you can just show up for your hobbies and passions that you'll find the greatest sense of fulfillment and accomplishment.

I recently went with my Dad to buy his dream car. It was really fulfilling for me to watch him live out a dream that he had delayed for decades in order to give our family the things that were important to us.

As I was sitting with the twenty-something salesperson, we were swapping stories about what we like to do in our lives. Over the course of three hours, I shared with him a few things that I do in Colorado, and how I got my start in life. I'm not sharing this with you to "toot my own horn," but we were just getting to know each other and these came out through adventure and life stories that we were sharing with each other. Here's what I was happy to share about me.

FACTS ABOUT ME

 I started working as a construction worker and equipment operator out of college.

 I ran my own landscape construction company, and I was introduced to my wife of now thirteen years by one of my employees.

 We've travelled to many parts of the United States, Canada, Mexico, the Caribbean, the British Virgin Islands, Central America, and went on an adventure to Thailand together.

 I love spending time with my daughter and watching her do gymnastics.

 I love showing her the ropes of self-defense, hiking, nature, reading, and how to understand and work with animals.

 I love living in Fort Collins, Colorado, were we get to ski, hike, bike, play, and enjoy some of the best craft beer in the country.

 I bow-hunt in the mountains of Colorado.

 I'm lucky enough to have friends from all over the world.

 I've been published and have contributed content to six major news outlets for my profession.

 I love to travel to Wisconsin. It's one of my favorite places.

 I have scrabble competitions with my wife.

 I have a brown belt in Brazilian Jiu Jitsu and still train regularly at my age.

As they had completed the papers on the car sale, and we were walking out and shaking hands, the salesman looks at me and says, "Holy cow! I feel so inadequate after sitting here and listening to all of your stories because I don't do anything that you do with the intensity and at the pace that you do it." Then he looked at me and said, "How do you do it all? You're...like superhuman. I need to get off the couch and get going!," Then he laughed nervously.

My reply was instant and from the heart. All I said was, "Buddy, it's available to you too. I'm no better than you. Heck, I'm no better than anyone. I just choose to show up everyday. Even on the days I don't feel like it, and there are plenty, I still show up and choose to pursue what I'm passionate about. That's it.

It's a choice, and you can have it too. Instead of habitually watching TV or spending time in bars, I'm trying to make it happen. I'm steering my life towards the things that excite me. I am driving my energy towards my passions."

It's nothing that I feel like others can't do. It's just that I've tried to make the effort to show up on a daily basis and have some kind of control regarding the direction of my life.

The point of the story is, I am the product of my daily discipline. Others around me choose to let life happen to them, and then react to it. I've been fortunate enough to have the daily discipline to go in the direction of my passions.

> "Your greatest self has been waiting your whole life;
> don't make it wait any longer."
> ~ Dr. Steve Maraboli

As you are beginning to reshape or shape the third chapter of your life, remember, that the act of just showing up on a daily basis is all that you need to accumulate a long list of accomplishments in your retirement.

Even though you're retired, I encourage you to develop that daily discipline. After a few years of retirement, so many people get caught up in the expectation that they don't HAVE to do anything. After forty years of working, they no longer have goals. They no longer *have* to do anything.

Your Personal Strategy Session

If you want true fulfillment in retirement, you do have continue to challenge yourself physically, mentally, and spiritually. As you continue to grow in retirement you'll give yourself the fun of bringing something new and fresh to the dinner table when you eat with your spouse. If you're divorced or your spouse has passed and you have children or grandchildren, you'll be able to share something about your life that is fresh and exciting.

It's when you do your daily exercises, and you tally what you did the day before, that you can be proud that you're out there accomplishing those goals. Be proud that you created those goals, and you made them happen. If you weren't successful in accomplishing all of the things you set out to do that day, go back and reevaluate what prevented you from being able to check that goal off your list and try again the next day.

CHAPTER 17
THE POWER OF THE OPEN HEART

I shared with you earlier in the book, when I'm in an interview with a potential client, one of the things I like to do first is to get to know whom I may be working with. I'm not talking about just their finances. That's typically the last thing we talk about. The first thing I like to do is to know more about whom I'm sitting across the table from. What makes that person or couple tick? Where do they want to be in retirement?

As we're doing this exercise, while talking about what they want to do in retirement and how they view the purpose of their money, people have opened up to me and shared, that they lack the personal connection to their family that they once had, because they been successful at cultivating strong children, or their children have moved away, and they don't have that daily connection with their children or grandchildren.

It's inspired me to really continue to develop the relationships I have with my wife, my daughter, and my close friends. This has brought my immediate family closer together, and strengthened the connections I have with my friends. With the help of other brilliant people, I've learned the power of the open heart.

When I hear clients come into my office talking about the lack of connection they have in their lives regularly. I often ask what prevents them from having a good connection in their relationships.

How do we redesign personal relationships? This is a tough one, but it's really important for getting the most fulfillment from retirement. I like to think of it in terms of the power of the open heart. Not everyone reading this is going to be open to this, but I believe the power of the open heart is dramatically underrated. You can use this power to strengthen relationships with others, if they too have open hearts, even though those people aren't geographically close to you.

In retirement, you may find it challenging to get what you want out of fulfilling relationships with your spouse, your children and/or your friends. One of the things I like to do with my family is to play games that build connection.

Wouldn't It Be Nice

If you're passionate about having fulfilling relationships with family, try some simple games I like to play. Eric Edmeades , creator of Wildfit, gave a speech I attended. He talked about a game that he likes to play with his wife to build connection and learn more about his family. It's called "wouldn't it be nice." He encouraged us to play this game because it gets us in the dream mode where you feel that anything is possible.

I love to play this game, in a playful way, with my wife and my daughter, because it helps us to dream together. If we're doing mundane driving on a long trip, we can break up the monotony by playing wouldn't it be nice…if we were there already. Wouldn't it be nice if we could fly rather than drive.

You can use the "wouldn't it be nice" game in your own personal life by starting a game with your spouse by starting with:

- Wouldn't it be nice if I were a brilliant painter.
- Wouldn't it be nice if I were a fast reader.

- Wouldn't it be nice if I had the dream car I always wanted but never had the courage to buy.
- Wouldn't it be nice if people around me understood me more.
- Wouldn't it be nice if we had a stronger family connection.

This game is responsible for our incredible family adventure I would have never dreamed we would actually complete together. In the fall of 2016, my wife and I were playing wouldn't it be nice and I said, "wouldn't it be nice if we went on a family adventure to Thailand for thirty days.

Low and behold, seven months later, that dream became a reality. If I hadn't played that game with my wife, I never would have had the courageous fun of dreaming an adventure like that with my wife. Playing that game and putting dreams into words helped my wife to understand what was in my heart… as a dream.

Through playing that game, I found out what was in her heart regarding wanting to have that connection to adventure with our family. I encourage you to try it with your family too. Wouldn't it be nice if once a month we had a big family dinner and we shared all of the positive things we love about each other and have done with one another? Wouldn't it be nice if we talked about what we are aiming for in our lives in the next year? Wouldn't it be nice if we all understood each other and respected each other just a little more than we do today?

Through those conversations, we've been able to carve out the time to do fun things together and learn about each other. Through those open hearted conversations we've been able to open up to each other, dream together, understand each other more and help each other make those dreams come true.

WOULDN'T IT BE NICE...

Wouldn't it be nice if I were a brilliant painter...

Wouldn't it be nice if I were a fast reader...

Wouldn't it be nice if I had the dream car I always wanted but never had the courage to buy...

Wouldn't it be nice if people around me understood me more...

Wouldn't it be nice if we had a stronger family connection...

_____

_____

_____

_____

_____

_____

_____

_____

Do You Really Know Me

There is another game we like to play occasionally that Eric Edmeades shared in his talk called, "Do you really know me?" This game takes courage, because the point is to share with the person you are playing with what is really in your heart. This is a great game if you really want to develop a greater understanding of your spouse, children and grandchildren. It's amazing the things you can learn about someone you think you already know.

The obvious benefit of playing this game is to really develop an understanding of who you really are. Here's the rub: It takes great courage and a non-judgmental attitude to give and receive the most of yourself and your partner when playing this game. I encourage you to open the game with playful hidden facts about yourself, but if you really want to go deep, make sure you are in a secure and supportive scenario and in a clear, happy mind.

The biggest takeaway from this chapter and these exercises is that I encourage you to seize the day today. As we've been exploring in this book, life is precious and short.

> ## Why now? Why this day?

While writing this book, I had a text from a very special friend, who had recently retired, one morning, wanting to get together for lunch. Knowing that I would be leaving for our family adventure for a month and knowing there was no way I could meet up with him any other day that week, we found a place to meet a few hours later.

We hadn't seen each other for months because life gets in the way. As with most good friends, when we connected it was as if time never separated us.

We caught up on the past, laughed, and talked about his retirement. He shared with me all of the emotions that he was going through early in his retirement. He was relieved of not having to go to work everyday. He missed the people and the culture of the workplace he worked so hard to create and had a tremendous positive impact on.

He at times already felt the pains of being isolated. He was excited about some upcoming travel with his wife. He shared that on some days he was flat-out bored and struggled finding new things to do.

We talked about his need to find a new passion, something that would excite him like his work, which he loved. He talked about some of his passions he was deciding to pursue. We even talked about this book and how our conversation was very relevant to his life personally because he was living the excitement and struggles of retirement.

I'm grateful I had the courage to share with him how much his friendship had meant to my wife and me, over the years, and how lucky we were to have him as a friend, and he shared the same with me. We laughed and talked about how we were going to connect when my family returned from our adventure to Thailand, and we imagined how we were going to shake things up and create some more exciting times in our life together later this summer and fall.

That lunch conversation was on a Wednesday late in June 2017. I got the news that my dear friend had passed away in a tragic accident just three days later on a Saturday. Although me heart is heavy, knowing my friend has moved on, I do feel grateful that the friendship between his family, my wife and me allowed for some very open-hearted conversations about our past together and the gratitude we have for each other. I'm even more grateful that we had seized the day to share open hearts.

I'm encouraging you to seize this day. Don't let tomorrow pass you by. Don't let the opportunity to build stronger relationships with your family by playing these simple games. They don't have to be deep and heavy conversations. Make the games light hearted and fun, but don't delay.

Recap

In this chapter we talked about how to take action finding your true passions in life. Some of you may know exactly the passions you want to pursue in the third chapter in life. For those of you who need some help, I would encourage you to take Janet Attwood's "Passion Test". Once you're able to drill down on what your greatest passions are, you can develop a clearer list of the daily habits you need to create that will help you get there.

Designing new habits requires honest self-evaluation. You can increase your ability to avoid the distractions that will take you off of your passion path by knowing what those distractions are, how to avoid them, and how to create a morning ritual that can keep you laser focused on getting the most out of the third chapter of your life. You have a powerful example of the daily discipline I have used for years to systematically avoid distractions and help me achieve what I'm most passionate about.

When taking action toward your passions the most important tool for success is seeing your small daily victories, by checking off your daily accomplishments.

Success leads to confidence and confidence leads to success.

You may feel a lack of connection to your family and friends in retirement. An open heart is a powerful tool that can help you redevelop those connections. It takes courage to have an open heart, but the rewards certainly outweigh the missed opportunities of not having heartfelt fulfilling conversations and experiences.

Your Personal Strategy Session

Don't delay. Start now and take the steps to identify what you're most passionate about. Develop the new routine that will help get you the most fulfillment. Act on your life. Don't react to life. Use the determination you had while working to get what you want in your retirement. Have the courage to have open-hearted conversations to really find meaningful relationships and experiences with those you love.

FULLFILLMENT AND WHY

CHAPTER 18
WHY DO WE NEED IT?

"I went into the woods because I wished to live deliberately,
to front only the essential facts of life, and see if I could not
learn what it had to teach, and not, when I came to die,
discover that I had not lived."
~ Henry David Thoreau

So what is all this fulfillment and "living a life true to ourselves" stuff about anyway?

What really creates fulfillment in our lives? What's the recipe that really gets our engines revved up and flowing? The answer is very similar to the way many of us go through the phases of Honeymoon; Staying at Home and Continuing Old Habits; and Chasing the Feeling of Being Full in our own unique way.

We all have the same basic needs for fulfillment, and we even create fulfillment in the same basic way, but our own experiences of fulfillment are unique to each of us individually. That's a really cool thing. We don't have to reinvent the recipe for fulfillment, but we do get to create it in our own special way.

I love that! It means that none of us really have to do anything during our lives in retirement that we don't really have to. You have every opportunity to live a life true to yourself because you don't have a boss to report to, a deadline to meet, a retirement to save for and vacation time to build. You have those basic needs met! Living in the Triangle of Success, you are really able to live a life true to yourself. You have the proof and now the permission that it's available to you!

Why create fulfillment & happiness in our lives?

Humans have evolved over time as members of communities. We've survived by sticking together. No matter what point in time, region of the world or culture, humans have not survived living independently.

The simple tasks of providing food, shelter, and protection were so difficult that we could not be successful alone. To survive as humans, we banded together for the benefit of each other's skills and presence. We were and are more successful providing food for each other and protecting each other as a unit. This success is what has given humans the opportunity to expand in greater ways.

Humans have always thrived by being responsible to each other. In both ancient and modern cultures, every single person in the community, tribe, or group has value. Children were responsible for helping with chores, taking care of animals, and helping to collect water and plants; young, middle-aged, and older adults provided food, protection, and shelter; and the elderly would do the same tasks as the adults, but they would also teach the young and provide guidance and wisdom from their experiences.

Creating Self-Worth In Retirement

These responsibilities give individuals a sense of purpose because the entire community needs each individual's contribution. Do you see how the following statements create worth in an individual's mind?

- My community needs me because I provide (fill in the blank).
- I get up every day to meet the responsibility of providing (fill in the bland) for people around me.
- I feel valued because the people around me need what I provide.

I believe we are victims, in a way, of our own successes. In the recent past, we have become more independent, less reliant, and more isolated than any other time in history. Even though we live in bigger cities, we are more isolated from close relationships and from being valued.

Think about the many people living in high-rise apartments, who are lacking real connection. Do they really know their neighbor? Are their neighbors relying on them for the food they eat? Or for the shelter they live in and for the safety they enjoy? Not really. Many people don't even have a connection to the person who provides their food or the place it comes from. If you live in a city and are buying your meals wrapped in plastic, is there any connection to that animal or to the field where the plants were grown? Not really. It came in on the back of a truck, given to you with the exchange of paper.

Have you seen anyone at a local grocery story or business get upset because the service wasn't fast enough? I believe it's because of the lack of connection to the service provider and the product. An appreciation for the responsibility of the person who provided the product or good is waning. Society is becoming disconnected in some areas of the world because rather than getting an appreciative smile or the satisfaction of seeing someone using the product you worked so hard to create, you simply get some numbers deposited into a bank account in exchange for our work.

Since the dawn of time, we have been animals that thrive under the weight of responsibility. We find value in providing for others around us. We find value in having purpose. Having to fulfill that responsibility is what gets us up in the morning with purpose.

Responsibility

Let me give you an example. Many men I know who have served in the military miss their military units. I've talked with many men, who, despite enduring the difficulties and horrors of war, have said they miss their time of service. They don't really miss the act of war, but they do miss the collective cohesiveness of their units.

When asked why, they almost all same the same thing, "We all had a responsibility to each other. We all relied on each other and needed each other. We were willing to live and DIE for each other." Wow! Talk about the feeling that your contributions and responsibilities have value! Talk about waking up with the feeling of purpose!

Even facing the harshest conditions and possibly death, these men had and have a deep sense of value and purpose for the other people in their unit. Even more interesting is that despite the fact that members of their unit had different-colored skin, spoke differently, had different religions, and came from different areas of the country, they all had a sense of responsibility to each other and for each other. Pretty amazing huh?!

That's powerful! I believe we can all learn a lesson from that.

Responsibility, purpose, and value are core ingredients for fulfillment.

Connection Can Defeat Depression

Call me silly, but I believe that depression is a relatively new phenomenon, especially in American culture. We have already talked about how retirees are being marginalized for lack of value, lack of contribution, and the thought they do not have much to offer. Families are spread out more than ever. We connect over the phone with our families and friends for ten minutes, instead of interacting with each other face-to-face. Have we sacrificed a true connection? I believe so. Our own success has caused humans to feel isolated and disconnected, leading to a higher incidence of depression, and the rabbit hole it drives us into.

So how do you undo this downward spiral of isolation, lack of purpose, lack of value and, ultimately lack of fulfillment in retirement life? Ready for it? Here goes: **by saddling yourself with responsibility.**

The Positivity Of Responsibility

Now before you get out the pitchfork and light the torches to come hunt me down, I know you may be near or in retirement. I know you most likely wish you could put work behind you for good. I'm encouraging you to do exactly that. Put your work behind you. What I'm talking about is taking on the responsibility of playfully living a life true to yourself.

Retirement life doesn't have to be about completely removing yourself from the weight of carrying a responsibility. In fact, it shouldn't. I hope you now understand why. It's a road to nowhere. I agree that it isn't easy to carry the weight of responsibility and to have people depending on you, but that ease bears a whole lot of negative side effects.

THE PITFALLS OF RETIREMENT

Little social interaction

Feelings that the best days are behind and gone

No valuable contribution to make

Lack of real purpose

> The reward of responsibility to others trumps all pain and suffering.
> This is how we create fulfillment!

I hope you can now see that life in retirement is about the reduction of the pain we had in the struggle to save for a stress-free retirement, but it's not about the loss of responsibility and purpose. You have to have a purpose and responsibility to create fulfillment and self-worth in your retirement life.

Responsibility and purpose are a part of being a person because it's in our nature. It's how we've survived over millions of years. Being responsible for each other and our community gives us value. Lack of responsibility and purpose affects our happiness, in the sense that it dampens our self-worth, and that's where we go wrong in our thoughts about retirement.

So much of the media and our own mental burnout from our working years has us thinking that retirement is about us checking out of responsibility and not carrying the weight of purpose. That's where the confusion about happiness hits us. Happiness in retirement is not about leaving our work to do nothing but exist waiting to die, chasing grandkids and over-indulging in food, or filling our voids with consumerism and lethargy.

Happiness in retirement *IS* about putting behind us the work we may not fully enjoy and ending the practice of having our schedules and responsibilities dictated to us. It is about being able to choose the responsibilities, the schedule we keep, and the people we want to be around that REALLY interest us. It's about choosing, a passion that we totally and completely get fired up about— a passion or interest that holds our attention and fills our spirit and inspires us to look forward to the next day, rather than wondering how we are going to fill our day with what is on TV or how the weather is going to be.

This is precisely the problem. How does the successful cardiologist go from saving lives everyday to checking into the golf course day after day and get the same fulfillment?

How does the mother, who has the most important job in the household, go from fulfilling the needs of her children everyday, to not being needed because her children are grown and having children of their own living across the country?

How does the engineer go from creating products and solving problems to reading the paper every day and watching junk on TV? Where is the comparable fulfillment in that life?

How does the teacher who positively affects change in the lives of her students everyday, find fulfillment from not exchanging ideas or sharing their love of teaching on a daily basis?

Your Personal Strategy Session

How do *you* go about replacing or finding a new source of fulfillment?

Visit www.TheRetirementDreammaker.com to get help answering the questions that will help you create greater fulfillment in your life and help you live a life true to yourself.

CHAPTER 19
RETIREMENT AS A REVOLUTION

> "It is not the strongest of the species that survives, nor the most intelligent, but the one most responsive to change."
> ~ Charles Darwin

*R*Evolution can seem like a scary term for many retirees. It sounds a lot like work! Who wants to work? Retirement isn't about work. You just got done with a lifetime of work! Who in their right mind would ever look at retirement as an evolution that requires effort, forethought and responsibility?

People who have lived busy lives away from work have an easier time transitioning into the retirement evolution. Work did not define them as a human. Their working lives were a part of their life, but life away from work was just as important. These are the people who pursued passions that interested them on a personal level.

I have a friend named Paul. Paul was a very successful self-employed businessman. I've always admired Paul because of his abundance of energy and the spark in his eye, a dedication to his family and community. Over the years, Paul and I have talked about how he developed his business and a life he enjoys.

Paul impressed upon me that business is business, but there is more to life. During his working years, he always seemed to be happily pursuing his passions of reading up on history, travelling to places that interested him, giving back to his community, and helping people in a meaningful way with his business skills.

Paul seemed to balance work and his personal passions with the greatest of ease. The truth is he worked very hard to not only build his business, but to carve out time from his busy schedule for his personal interests.

A few years ago, Paul retired, and he has been able to seamlessly transition away from work into a life full of growth by following his passions. To this day, he is continually evolving, and each time I see him he talks about the next challenges he plans to take on. That includes the new passions he's developing, the people he's helping, and the information he is learning and putting to use. He is using his time in retirement to grow and explore his physical capabilities as his body changes with age. He's expanding his emotions by connecting with his wife, children, grandchild and friends in more meaningful ways. Paul is also expanding spiritually through reading and having conversations with like-minded friends. He's very fulfilled, and he is truly enjoying the "third chapter" of his life.

RETIREMENT REVOLUTION

CHAPTER 20
THE BEST IS YET TO COME

"What would you attempt to do if you knew you could not fail?"
~ Robert H. Schuller

Wow! We've come a long way together. Let's recap the new awareness you have, the tools you possess and expand your vision of what's possible in the third chapter of your life.

We now know how it's easy to think that our life in retirement is unique to us and that we have little in common with other people in retirement. The reality is that we have much more in common than we are really aware of. In the context of the path we walk in retirement, people in the past have all gone through it pretty much the same way.

As people hit their retirement date milestone, many of those people experience "The Honeymoon" right away and are in vacation/party mode. Other people, who aren't as energized, get stuck staying at home and continuing their past habits. Many people also "chase the feeling of being full", rather than direct their life in a way true to themselves. I believe, from my experience working with pre-retirees and retirees for almost two decades that most people have no clue as to the difference in these and the different results the walk on these paths get them internally versus really living a life true to themselves.

Living a retirement life following any three of these paths may produce a sense of happiness in a person's life, I agree. I believe most people get unconsciously stuck here because they think they are happy.

We know from the statements of people receiving palliative care, this is not true at all. Simple happiness is not enough. In the end, true fulfillment is what matters to people in their lives.

> There is a profound difference between happiness and fulfillment in life.

However, most people believe they are one in the same. The truth is they are as different as ice cream and chocolate syrup topping. They are both deserts but totally different.

Vishen Lakhiani, author of *The Code Of The Extraordinary Mind*, beautifully articulates the differences. He says, "You can get happiness from a joint. But long-term happiness and fulfillment come from something more-the need to contribute, grow, and do meaningful things."

We explored how good people get fooled into thinking the traditional retirement construct is all that waits for them. You now understand there are some pitfalls waiting for you that can be avoided. The pitfalls that many good people fall into in retirement are:

- Little social interaction
- Feelings that the best days are behind and gone
- No valuable contribution to make
- Lack of real purpose

You now also know that there are many circumstance, situations and events that contribute to people getting stuck in these pitfalls. They include:

- Lack of money
- Lack of permission
- Health complications
- Isolation
- Waiting for milestones
- Feeling irrelevant or as if you have no value to give

Through the stories of Mark and Margaret, you have seen how these circumstances, situations, and events unfold in people's lives, and how they can get trapped in the traditional retirement construct.

Thankfully, by increasing your awareness of the traditional retirement construct, and by understanding the common pitfalls that pre-retirees and retirees fall into you are better able to identify them if and when they come up in your life. More importantly, you now have a better understanding of how to avoid them if and when they come up in your life.

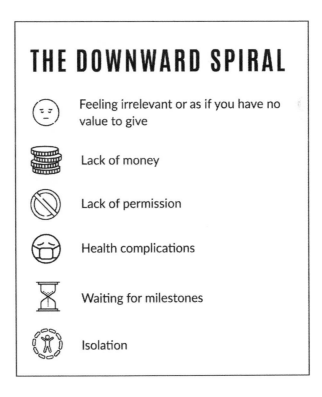

> We don't know what we don't know!

Well, now you know. So, keep your eyes open and "try not to step in it"!

I hope you have had a tremendous expansion in your understanding of what prevents good people from living a life true to themselves. They are simple pressures, but they are powerful.

Pressures and feelings you want to overcome are:

Familial Expectations/Constructs
Societal Pressures
Money – The perception of the lack of it
Our own daily habits
Lack of Direction
Apathy
Courage

How many of us have been stopped dead in our tracks from living a life true to ourselves because of these? My secret is out... I know I have! They are tough to overcome, but you *do* have the courage to overcome each and every one of these pressures and feelings.

The reason you want to overcome all of these is because when you can, you have something very powerful to use to your advantage. You unknowingly created it. It's the result of years of delayed gratification, disciplined saving, disciplined living, and dedicated work. You have the "Triangle of Success" to utilize in the pursuit of living a life true to yourself.

THE TRIANGLE OF SUCCESS

Personal/Professional
Life Skills

FULFILLMENT

Money   Time

Most people have no idea how powerful "The Triangle Of Success" is and how it can support them in their pursuit of living a life true to themselves. You do now!

There should be no other point in time in your life of greater abundance of money; personal and professional life skills; and time to go after your passions.

You now know that what is waiting for you in the third chapter of your life is happiness, excitement, value, contribution, and fulfillment! You are at the absolute pinnacle of time in your life to access information about your passions. From the comfort of your own home, you have the ability access information anywhere on the globe through the internet quickly and efficiently.

With our ability to travel to anywhere in the world, depression resulting from isolation should be a thing of the past. Traveling with a purpose can make the experience more exciting. Traveling with a purpose can also help us gain new insights about our passions from people anywhere we can imagine.

It doesn't matter if you live in the heartland, and your nearest neighbor is one mile away, or if you live in a big city high-rise, but you don't really know your neighbor, you can create connection with others in very real and meaningful way. We talked about the power of using the internet to connect to forums and online communities of people that have shared interests with you. The internet can be a powerful way to connect to existing communities that share your passions. The internet can also be a way to create a new community of people who share your interests, from anywhere in the world you can imagine.

Hopefully, through our stories of Moorie Boogart, Meg Skinner, and Grace Larson, you understand that you can get fulfillment at any point in time in your life and you're never too old to make a difference in people's lives.

In Chapter 7, I revealed the importance of shifting from 100 percent asset accumulation strategies to incorporate more asset preservation strategies into your retirement plan when you are near or in retirement. We talked about how you don't have to sacrifice safety for good returns—You can have both!

You now have a greater understanding of why these strategies and tools have been hidden from you or stigmatized by big banks and stockbrokers. They have no incentive to tell you about these strategies because, often, they would make less money if you used them *and* they lack the licensing to talk about them. Often, they make less money if you use them, which is why they don't get licensed to offer them and why wouldn't they try their hardest to demonize these strategies. Shame on them!

I revealed how and why the old construct of retirement planning leads to the feeling of uncertainty, anxiety, and mistrust. By shifting a large portion of your assets away from 100 percent asset accumulation to asset preservation strategies you can create more safety, a guaranteed income, and a sense of certainty in your life. By reducing your stress and anxiety about things you have very little control over (the stock market, news cycle, world events), you can give yourself permission to pursue a life true to yourself with less worry that your retirement savings are going to disappear overnight.

We reviewed the retirement structure I recommend for my private clients and how that structure can help you understand how each portion of your money is working for you inside of your retirement plan. To review, think of your money in terms of fulfilling three purposes:

Immediate money: the money you can access first thing in the morning if you need it.

Income producing money: the money needed to produce the income goal you have in retirement.

Legacy money: the money you can use to solve medical problems and/or finance a legacy for your family. This is the money to be used fund long-term health care insurance, which can help you fund treatment of medical problems, or, life insurance, which can help you with legacy gifting, and avoiding or reducing taxes.

This is a very simple and effective way to think of your money in terms of what purpose/goal your money accomplishing for you. You now have a greater understanding of how to reposition your assets in retirement away from the old construct for you and your family's benefit.

You have a greater understanding about the importance of working with an independent planning specialist and the difference between a suitability standard of care versus a fiduciary standard of care. Big banks, stockbrokers and sales agents, who can only offer one to four types of mutual funds or strategies often only have a suitability standard. It's important to work with a dually licensed (securities and insurance) adviser or firm, who must abide by the fiduciary standard of care, because they must be independent and have the ability to research the market and offer solutions tailored to your needs, rather than fitting your needs into what is available by the company or strategies they represent.

We reviewed the story of the disconnected investor. Our good friend Bruce fell into the trap of the disconnected investor the same way many good people do. Bruce felt intimidated to talk to his 401(k) adviser because the language used in his review meetings "were over his head". He never bothered to learn the basics of a Morningstar Report and his quarterly statements were complete gibberish to him. Not wanting to feel unintelligent, he blindly followed his advisers' and friends' recommendations, and like so many people, he lost a large amount of his retirement savings. He sold low and bought high. This led Bruce to having much less in retirement than he really deserved.

We also reviewed the story of the connected investor. Our friend, Amy, did have a little good luck. Her friend made a wise recommendation that she visit with a financial adviser. Although this was a stroke of good luck, Amy had the *courage* to act on the recommendation, and her life was much different. Although she endured the same circumstances in retirement as our friend, Bruce, her experience was much different. Amy shifted her retirement assets from 100 percent asset accumulation strategies to include more asset preservation strategies to provide safety of principle, guaranteed income. and decent returns. By being open to restructuring her retirement plan, Amy experienced much less anxiety enduring the tough times of 2007 and 2008. She created income that she could not outlive and had less worry about the uncertainty of things she had little or no control over and how they would affect her life in retirement. She created an income greater then she really needed without taking chances, AND she had extra income that helped her to live a life true to herself and pursue her passions.

Having a true connection and understanding of your retirement assets and plan is available to you to! Like Amy, you are going to need to have the courage to change how you think about your retirement plan AND you are going to have to invest some time in finding the people that can help you most effectively structure your plan in this way.

You now know you have a tremendous opportunity, and the tools, to change what retirement can mean to you and in your life. The traditional construct of retirement has been exposed, and you have the power to reshape your new construct of retirement. You don't have to fall into the same path of retirement as those before you and around you right now. Bronnie Ware revealed to us, through her work as a palliative caregiver, the biggest regret that people have in their retirement.

> **The biggest regret in people's lives, in palliative care, is they lacked the courage to "live a life true to themselves"**

That's painful for me to read those words. It's painful to me, because that pain of regret may have been completely avoided. I've done my best to help you understand the biggest regret that people have at the end of their lives. Hopefully, by increasing your understanding of the problem and how it happens to good people you avoid that regret in your life.

Your Personal Strategy Session

It's my hope that you are able to benefit from one of the greatest advantages I have in life through my role as a Retirement Planning Adviser. Through interviewing more than 1,000 pre-retirees and retirees over the years I benefit from witnessing the consequences of the poor choices people have made in life. I also see, first hand, the difficult situations people have endured in their life that lead to isolation, depression, insecurity, and uncertainty during their life in retirement. Should you choose to, you can get the benefit of evaluating all of the poor choices and bad circumstances that have cropped up in your life and how you can identify and/or avoid them. You now are able to observe the positive choices and situations that people create in their lives that can lead to excitement, opportunity, certainty, and fulfillment during life in retirement.

It's my privilege to share these lessons with you in hopes that you too will benefit and live a life in retirement with as much security, happiness, connection, and fulfillment as possible. My biggest hope is that the content on these pages will help you live a life true to yourself with as much ease and happiness possible.

CHAPTER 21
RESOURCES AVAILABLE TO YOU

"Start living your life fearlessly!"
~ Matthew Jackson

Let's take some time to expand your ideas about what's available to you when you consider how to start living a life true to yourself. You may be the big thinker and want to make an impact globally, or you may have a strong desire to pursue a passion that you've not been able to because of family and work responsibilities. It doesn't matter. I believe you will benefit greatly from the following pages in terms of understanding what is out there.

As I mentioned earlier, one of the most difficult challenges to overcome when beginning or finding yourself in retirement is getting going. Whether you lack direction, need help asking the question of what excites you, or need help understanding the different ways that you can get involved, getting started is the first step. I'd like to give you some examples that will answer these questions.

We're going to explore the question to provide answers from a 30,000-foot view, a 15,000-foot view and then a "street level" view.

If you're a "big picture" thinker and have a desire to make an impact globally, or if you want to make the biggest impact in what interests you around the globe, I'd like to open your mind to a couple of possible ways that you could get involved or build a community of other like-minded people that may help you with your passion.

30,000-Foot View

Meet Hero^X

Hero^X.com is a website that allows innovators to search or create crowdsourcing challenges. Hero^x offers companies and individuals the ability to solve problems or provide solutions to companies and people for prize money.

From the "About Us" page.
"HeroX was co-founded in 2013 by XPRIZE founder Peter Diamandis, challenge designer Emily Fowler and entrepreneur Christian Cotichini as a means to democratize the innovation model of XPRIZE.
Hero^X exists to enable anyone, anywhere in the world, to create a challenge that addresses any problem or opportunity, build a community around that challenge and activate the circumstances that can lead to a breakthrough innovation." www.herox.com ~ about page
Some of Hero^x's most successful crowdsourcing projects include:
Space Poop, Forbes Under 30 $1M Change the World Competition, Autism Speaks House to Home Prize, Integra Gold Rush Challenge
If you are a "big picture" thinker this site may help search for challenges that interest you and if you'd like help solving a particular challenge, you have the opportunity to create challenge to inspire innovation.

www.herox.com

Meet GoFundMe

GoFundMe is the #1 fundraising platform, raising more resources than anywhere else on the planet. GoFundMe gives individuals the opportunity to donate and raise money for their passion and interests. If you have a desire to see where you're money goes and to see exactly how it helps people, causes, and places that you are passionate about, then you need to explore this website.

From the About Us page.

"Launched in 2010, GoFundMe is the world's largest social fundraising platform, with over $3 billion raised so far. With a community of more than 25 million donors, GoFundMe is changing the way the world gives.

Key Points

- Mobile-Friendly Campaigns
- No penalties for missing goal
- GoFundMe Mobile App
- No deadlines or goal requirements
- Five-Minute Email Support
- You can keep every donation you receive

There are countless opportunities to donate and your mind is the only limit on what you can create interest to raise money for.

www.gofundme.com

Meet Kiva

Kiva is an international non-profit connecting people around the globe through lending. The company has helped to create more than $1.01 billion in loans and has a more-than 97 percent repayment rate. They have helped more than 2.5 million people in eighty-four countries connect to more than 1.6 million lenders.

From the "About us" page:

"By lending as little as $25 on Kiva, anyone can help a borrower start or grow a business, go to school, access clean energy or realize their potential. For some, it's a matter of survival, for others it's the fuel for a life-long ambition. 100% of every dollar you lend on Kiva goes to funding loans. Kiva covers costs primarily through optional donations, as well as through support from grants and sponsors."

If you are the type of "big picture" thinker that likes to use money to "grow" people and things, check this site out. There are many categories of interest and a lot of opportunity to help.

www.kiva.org

These are a few of the organizations that can open your eyes to what is possible, when thinking about helping people anywhere on the globe. I hope you can see that through these types of organizations you can choose to join a community of like-minded people, create a community like-minded people, and affect a community people anywhere you can possibly imagine to help solve a myriad of problems.

15,000-Foot View

Meet Justin Wren of Fight For The Forgotten

I first heard about Justin Wren through my interest in mixed martial arts (MMA). Justin is a gigantic man who is tough as nails, with the will of a lion and the heart of a teddy bear.

From the "Who We Are" page.

"After a life-changing experience in 2011, Justin founded Fight for the Forgotten, a non-profit dedicated to securing land, freedom, and clean water for the formerly enslaved Mbuti Pygmy tribe in the Ituri rainforest of the Democratic Republic of the Congo. In 2015, Water4 helped him expand beyond the DRC to bring clean water and economic security to thousands across the region."

"The goal of our programs is to leave behind a growing, self-sustaining, missional Christian social enterprises that address the full needs of communities with regard to sustainable water access solutions, health and hygiene promotion, addressing and proclaiming the good news and catalyzing holistic transformation that comes from the presence of Jesus in the world."

Regardless of your religious affiliation, I'm sure we can all agree that access to clean drinkable water is a cause to be passionate about.

Justin Wren's story of creating Fight For The Forgotten is an inspirational story of how one man, through his passion of people, created his own community, enlisted the help of other like-minded people and is creating fulfillment in a significant way.

http://www.water4.org/fightfortheforgotten

Meet Taylor Conroy of Change Heroes

I heard about Taylor in November of 2016. I was instantly inspired by Taylor during a talk he gave letting people know that they can make a big impact in the world by enlisting just a little bit of help from friends.

"Change Heroes was born from a life changing trip. When our founder Taylor Conroy returned from Kenya, he was changed. He saw firsthand where his charitable donation went to, and the impact the funds had on the lives of school children. But most importantly he knew that he wanted to give this gift to hundreds of more people just like him." www.changeheros.com- homepage

From the "About Us" page.

"United For Change. Driven By Impact. We are a community of passionate individuals who are united by our desire for change. The kind of change that drives real impact in the world.

As a community we've raised well **over $3 million** across 40 different countries.

And the best part is that we have been able to fly hundreds of our fundraisers to their impact site to see firsthand the change they've created and to connect with the thousands of individuals that need our help.

With the help of Change Heroes' video-first fundraising technology platform, our charity partners raise four to five times their typical amount while building a strong millennial donor base. Our online, peer-to-peer fundraising technology creates a unique opportunity for charities to raise more funds and build a recurring donor base."

If you would like to engage in peer-to-peer funding of a cause or passion you have interest in, www.changeheros.com gives you a unique opportunity to make a big impact globally, nationally, and locally. Again, your mind is the only limit on what you can do here.

www.changeheros.com

Street Level View

I'm going to spend a lot more time on the "Street Level" view. As I review these examples of passions commonly followed to create fulfillment for people in retirement, I invite you to open your mind to the strategies that I'm revealing to you that create the opportunities to pursue passions no matter where you live. I'm keenly aware that many of you reading this book may feel limited because you have a physical handicap, live in rural area, and/or really are passionate about your locality.

You may find yourself asking some simple questions when thinking about living a life true to yourself.

Person 1: I know exactly what I want to do, but I'd like to explore my passion by learning from and with others.

Person 2: I have an idea of what living a life true to myself looks like, but what else is out there that might interest me?

Person 3: I never thought I would be able to retire and I need help discovering what living a life true to me really means.

I've provided you with examples that should help you to open your mind to what is available to you, regardless of your situation. It's my hope that you can apply these principles to your life if you have the ability and desire to travel, a desire to stay local, and/or a lack of local resources to pursue a life true to yourself. I hope you can frame these examples in ways that you can apply to your life individually.

Before we journey down this road, I'd like to remind everyone of some very sage advice, best offered by author and photographer Carol Roullard in a *Business Insider* article, "The whole idea about retirement is that you now control how you spend your time. Make sure whatever you choose, you can afford to do it. That way you can continue to be 'retired' rather than forced to get another job. I retired on a Friday and on Monday, my husband and I started writing a book together. We just released our fifth book together and I started printing my fine art photography. When asked what we do for a living, we stopped saying we were retired. Instead we say we changed careers."

I hope her words resonate with you. She and her husband are focused on staying retired and have turned a life of passion, living true to themselves, into a smart business opportunity. As I mentioned in the previous chapters, life in retirement is not about checking out of responsibility. It can be a life of responsibility you choose to enjoy and create fulfillment from.

In the same article, web designer Alan N. Canton went on to give some very insightful perspectives. "The retirement 'job' should be the one you've always wanted to do or try. It is not about the money you will make, but the memories you will have.

"So often people think they should be doing something to help others. That's fine. But this is a time in life to put yourself 'first' and do whatever it is that you've always wanted to do."

"I've always been a techie. It paid well. But I've always wanted to be an artist. It didn't pay well (or at all!). Now I get to be both as a web designer."

I absolutely love his perspective. He seems to be living very comfortably in his "Triangle of Success". He has taken advantage of the fact that his skill set is at a very high level. He's chosen to leverage his skills (web design) with his passion (art). He has nothing but time to develop the artistic side of his business AND the money is a side benefit for him. What a retirement lifestyle success story!

In the final example shared in this article, I'd like to draw your attention to Lee Gale Gruen. She shares an inspiring story of completely switching gears in retirement and found a passion to keep her excited in life!

Her story is truly inspiring: "After retiring from my 37-year career as a probation officer, I attended an acting class for seniors for three years with my father starting when I was 60 and he was 85. We performed scenes I wrote in six class showcases before live audiences. As a result, I went on to become a professional actress in my senior years. Then, I became an author when I wrote a recently published memoir about it called, 'Adventures with Dad: A Father and Daughter's Journey Through a Senior Acting Class.' I'm now also a speaker as I give talks about my book and to inspire baby boomers and seniors to find a passion as a motivation to embrace life. My 'second act' keeps me vital and dynamic, and makes me excited about life."

Cooking passion

Meet Traveling Spoon

If you enjoy travelling, but are intimidated to travel to different places because of the lack of connection to locals, here's a brilliant way that you can have instant connection to people in a new place all while pursuing your passion of cooking. I love this opportunity because this website not only offers you the way to have instant connection to like-minded people, but helps you to have authentic experiences in a new place.

From the "About us" page.

"Traveling Spoon is like having a friend's mom cook you a home cooked meal in every country you visit. Traveling Spoon connects travelers with local, vetted hosts to share the joy of a homemade meal in their home and learn about their cultural and culinary traditions passed down through generations."

"To help you experience local cuisine while traveling, Traveling Spoon offers in-home meals with our hosts. In addition, we also offer in-home cooking experiences as well as market visits as an add-on to many of the meal experiences. All of our hosts have been vetted to ensure a safe and delightful culinary experience."

Visit www.travelingspoon.com to travel with a "foody" purpose.

Supporting Others Dealing With Cancer

Meet Imerman's Angels

If cancer has affected your life and you would like to get involved in supporting others fighting this horrible disease Imermanangels.org can help you pursue the passion of supporting others.

From the "About us" page.

"Their Mission: To provide personalized connections that enable one-on-one support among cancer fighters, survivors and caregivers. Through our unique matching process, Imerman's Angels partners anyone, any age, any gender, anywhere and any cancer type seeking support with someone just like them – a "Mentor Angel". A Mentor Angel is a cancer survivor or caregiver who most importantly has faced the same type of cancer.

Our service is absolutely free and helps anyone touched by any type of cancer, at any cancer stage level, at any age, living anywhere in the world.

These one-on-one relationships give a cancer fighter or caregiver the chance to ask personal questions and get support from someone who has been there before. Mentor Angels can lend support and empathy and help cancer fighters and caregivers navigate the system, determine their options and create their own support systems. Frequently, caregivers experience feelings similar to those of the person facing cancer. Mentor Angels can relate while being sensitive to the experience and situation."

Visit http://www.imermanangels.org/ to learn how you can grow your passion of helping others in your community.

Music Passion

I've spoken with a lot of pre-retirees and retirees who have had a serious passion for listening to and performing music but have had a hard time getting started learning an instrument. There are plenty of resources to learn a new instrument if you live in a big city or town.

Meet Guitar Center

If you can find a Guitar Center in your local area, they are a great resource to learn all types of instruments. Guitar Center provides music lessons for many more instruments other than the guitar. You can visit them at www.GuitarCenter.com

Meet YouTube

So what if you live in an area that doesn't have any resources for hiring a professional music teacher? Check out YouTube! There is seemingly an unlimited amount of videos on how to play any type of instrument with any type of instructor. You can simply type www.YouTube.com, into your internet browser, then type in the instrument you are interested in playing, and you're on the path to learning the instrument you are interested in.

Sara Lawrence-Lightfoot shared a really cool story in her *Wall Street Journal* article published on December 22, 2014 and titled, "How To Find Your Passion In Retirement."

She describes the life of a 62-year-old jet-setting entrepreneur. Despite the fact that this man was in international businessman and huge success, he had a desire for something different. Sara reveals, "Music has always been the thing that made him feel the most alive, and he had always been curious to know the 'logic and design' behind jazz music, the basic structures that allowed for improvisation. So even though he is a face-to-face kind of guy, he decided to 'cross the border into cyberspace.'

Sara goes on to explain, "Not only does the learning online require a 'different kind of discipline' and a 'private kind of accountability,'" it also seems to combine the odd sensation of intimacy and anonymity with his long-distance professor.

In cyberspace, he experiences a new kind of creativity, a new way of learning, and renewed passion. He feels freer to ask "dumb" questions, freer to take risks, freer to fail. He says, "Cyberspace is my new frontier." Grinning, he shifts metaphors, "I feel like a kid in a candy shop!" Work crosses over into play. The distance between New Delhi and New York City disappears into nothing."

"This entrepreneur feels himself drawn back home, to the echoes from his childhood, to the music he loves that knows no geographic boundaries."

What I hope you learn from this story is that no matter your geographic location, where you are isolated (on a farm with the nearest neighbor one mile away or in a corporate jet), there are opportunities and resources available to pursue a life true to yourself. This is a brilliant example of courage and open-mindedness. Sara does a brilliant job of strengthening my point that only your mind can limit what you do in retirement.

If you're inspired by this example and want to develop a life full of music, you can increase your connection to other like-minded musicians in online chat forums by searching your favorite internet search engine (Google, Yahoo, Bing, etc) and simply typing the subject "musician forum". You'll have a ton of options to choose from. Simply click on the description of a site that interests you, put on some of your favorite music, and click around the site to see what you discover.

To see more ways to inspire you to live a life true to yourself visit: www.TheRetirementDreammaker.com . We are constantly updating for your benefit.

"25 side gigs you can start in retirement", authored by Katie Little [2] offers more insight on people that want to have a reason to get out of bed in the morning. She addresses the idea of saddling yourself with responsibility, in a positive way, which we discussed earlier, and how continue to feel relevant in retirement, the community value concept I introduced in chapter 23.

Katie writes, "Driving this trend are three things: Retirees want to create a financial safety net as Americans live longer than ever, they want to pursue something meaningful and they want to avoid being bored."

In the article, Nancy Collamer, author of "Second-Act Careers: 50+ Ways to Profit from Your Passions During Semi-Retirement", reveals "what are some second act gigs that are tailor made for these retirees? Experts shares some of their top picks:

1. **Consultant**- By the time older Americans retire, they have accumulated substantial knowledge in their career, skills that they can turn into a side business with flexible hours. This is *one of the points of the Triangle of Success. Your personal and professional skills sets are most likely at their pinnacle.*

2. **Interim Executive**- There are now professional services firms that can place people in temporary executive positions," Collamer said. These

temporary execs typically earn a good rate and handle meaty assignments, she said.

3. Uber drivers- Ride apps offer the ultimate convenience: Workers can turn them on when they have extra time to work and turn them off when they want to be off the clock. Another bonus: The job can be very social for seniors who want to get out of the house.

4. Peace Corps- A full 7 percent of Peace Corps volunteers are over age 50. This could be a good fit for retirees who are ready to embark on a completely new adventure for their second act.

5. Personal historian- Lovers of history and writing can marry the two as personal historians, who help customers write their memoirs.

6. Life-cycle celebrant- These celebrants serve as officiant at important life moments, like weddings. "For someone who loves being around weddings or around important life moments or if they like to do research, that can be a fun idea," Collamer said.

7. Entrepreneurial support- With so many people branching out on their own, offering support services can be a flexible business retirees can begin. "Typically they're very skilled at core businesses, but it's all the other tasks they need to handle their business effectively," Collamer said.

8. Bookkeeper- Number-crunching seniors might want to look into offering bookkeeping services.

9. Web designer- In today's internet-centric world, having an informative and up-to-date business website is essential, and retirees with web design skills can sell their talent.

10. Virtual assistant- You can always make more money, but time? That's a scarce commodity for any businessman. Offering virtual assistant skills fits into many semi retirees' desire for flexibility.

11. Translator- Speak a foreign language? Your skills could be in high demand by businesses with entrepreneurs who don't have the skill.

12. Adjunct professor- Try going back to where it all started: college. "It can be very gratifying work for people. It's an opportunity for them to share their expertise and mentor a new generation of students," Collamer said.

13. Tutor- Teach the next generation of little Einsteins by offering your knowledge.

14. Senior services- As the boomer generation ages, there is a huge opportunity to provide services for them, such as home modification or moving logistics as a senior move manager.

15. Passion projects- Hannon recommended brainstorming a business idea from an existing sport or hobby. She cited the example of a woman who turned her love of sewing into a business making pillows out of old wedding dresses.

16. Tax preparer- Every year, it seems like the tax code gets more complicated with new credits to take and rules to remember. People with tax preparation skills will find their skills in high demand, especially come tax time, and companies like H&R Block stress the ability for their employees to have flexible hours.

17. Pet groomer- The pet business is big and only getting bigger. Pet walkers are another potential encore business opportunity.

18. Professional organizer- Professional organizer and best-selling author Marie Kondo has helped bring professional organization to the forefront.

19. Mediator~ Facing potentially sky-high legal bills, many opposing parties instead opt for mediation rather than drag disputes out in court. This presents an opportunity for people who have good conflict resolution skills. For more information on becoming one, check out the National Association of Certified Mediators.

20. Seamstress/Tailor~ Skills like sewing are not as common as they used to be. If you are especially handy in this arena, you might be cut out for a side gig as a seamstress or tailor.

21. Grant proposal writer~ Grant writing is highly specialized and can be time consuming, so people who specialize in it can be real value-adds to grant seekers. Check out the Grant Professionals Association for more information.

22. Specialty tour operator~ Ideal for people who live near tourist meccas, opening a specialty tour business can help people marry interests in a topic with social interaction and even some exercise.

23. Nonprofit worker~ Getting in touch with a nonprofit you already volunteer with or with another whose cause is interesting to you can be a great way to find a fulfilling way to fill the extra hours.

24. Babysitter or nanny~ With many families headed by single parents or two-income earners, parents are more time-strapped than ever and reliant on caregiving services.

25. Plant nursery worker~ Semi-retirees with a green thumb might be interested in this one. Bonus: These jobs can offer outside time, social interaction and exercise.

Setting Your Pace

I'd like to offer some words of advice to those of you who may incorporate turning a passion into living a life true to yourself. If you find yourself turning the passion into something that saddles you with responsibility in a positive way, by providing connection to community, value, relevance, make sure you do it on your terms.

> I encourage you set boundaries and stay within those boundaries to the best of your ability.

For example, if you love kids and decide to offer baby-sitting services, or if your kids enlist your help in watching the grandchildren while your kids are working or playing, do it in a way that fits into your time schedule

I know from first-hand experience that when you are using your passion to help others (free of charge or building a clientele)it can be tempting for them to ask more and more of your time. You don't want to develop a feeling that your passion is becoming like the work you retired from. By setting expectations and boundaries and keeping them, you are more likely to really enjoy what you're doing in your life. I encourage you to stay focused on maintaining balance and pure bliss of what you're doing to live a life true to yourself.

Meet "MeetUp.com"

This is a great destination if you feel isolated in any way, which we all do from time to time. Meetup helps you to create or join a community of like-minded people. Meetup is a valuable tool to start, grow, learn, and share the life you are living true to yourself with others in your area.

From the "About us" page.

"Meetup brings people together in thousands of cities to do more of what they want to do in life. It is organized around one simple idea: when we get together and do the things that matter to us, we're at our best. And that's what Meetup does. It brings people together to do, explore, teach and learn the things that help them come alive.

For example, people run marathons, thanks to running Meetups. They write, thanks to writing Meetups. They change their careers, thanks to career Meetups. Because at Meetups, people welcome each other. They talk, help, mentor, and support each other – all in pursuit of moving their lives forward."

www.Meetup.com

Challenging Yourself

One of the challenges I wanted to accomplish in this book was to make sure I provided ways for everyone to create, find, and build connection. First, you need to be able to identify the powerful negative spiral isolation can drive anyone to. Then, you need to know you have resources available to overcome that obstacle. However, I want to remind you that it's up to you to challenge your courage. You are going to have to take a chance and step into the temporary unknown. I say the unknown is temporary from personal experience.

Do you remember the story I shared with in you in chapter 18 regarding how I like to create connections when I travel through training in Brazilian Jiu Jitsu? Well, just know that it took courage for me to step out of my comfort zone, including walking into a place where people are waiting to ring your neck or twist your joints in ways that aren't natural and to smile and be open to engaging in conversations and an activity with people I've never met. Honestly, it's very tough for me, but I've found the more I step into the unknown, the more comfortable I am with it. The satisfaction I get from stepping into the unknown and creating new friendships and learning new perspectives is something that fulfills me in ways that... well... you need to experience for yourself too!

Now it's time for you to think about how to get started. If you'd like a simple action plan to help get your feet pointed in the right direction or help creating an action plan or if you'd like to be a part of an online community of people living a life true to themselves, visit www.RetirementWealthEvolution.com to get started on the most up-to-date action plan for shaping a life true to yourself.

CHAPTER 22
MY WISH

> "Your talent is God's gift to you.
> What you do with it is your gift back to God."
> ~ Leo Buscaglia

I firmly believe there is a reason this book crossed your path at this point in time in your life. It's my wish for you, that the content in these pages has expanded your understanding of what is possible to you in the third chapter of your life. As the cliché goes, knowledge is power!

I wish for you to have a greater understanding of the challenges and possibilities of structuring a solid retirement plan for the benefit of creating more confidence and ease in your financial life. You now know it is possible to create a powerful retirement plan that will last through tough times.

I wish for you to believe that living a life true to yourself is possible and that you give yourself the permission to do so, regardless of what your family expects of you, what your friends tell you, and what the media depicts to you.

I wish for you to feel comfortable resourcing the content in these pages over and over again to draw knowledge and insight on how to get started living a life true to yourself. Then I want you to maintain that focus, no matter the distractions and obstacles that come into your path.

I wish that the courage you find to take the action required to live a life true to yourself inspires others, of all ages, to live their life in the same way. This knowledge is now your responsibility. Even if you don't take action, your awareness has been expanded. Share that knowledge with others around you, so that they may have a better opportunity of squeezing the absolute most fulfillment out of their lives by living a life true to themselves.

I wish for you to know just how valuable you are and how people around you benefit from your knowledge and skills. You do have a greater opportunity, at this point in your life, to make significant contributions to your community. It doesn't matter if you perceive them as small or large. Everyone benefits from seeing your open heart shine and watching you being all that you can be.

Matthew Jackson

ACKNOWLEDGEMENTS

Reflecting on the journey of creating the content in these pages, it's humbling to think of the people who have contributed to its energy in their own special way.

Gratitude, thankfulness, and love to my wife, Victoria. I have so much gratitude for your love and support. Your special note of encouragement at the beginning of this project filled my heart with so much fire. You inspire and support me to be better every day.

To my daughter Ava, thank you for showing me the beauty and love in this world through the eyes of an open heart. You are an amazing example of living a life true to yourself. You're a bright shooting star.

To my mother, Irene S. Lawler and my uncle, Ralph J. Santori. The loss of you on this planet inspired me to take the chance of putting my heart on paper, so that others may benefit. I miss you both every day.

My sincere gratitude, thanks, and love to the remarkable team of Dr. Neeta Bhushan and Ajit Nawalkha. The energy we created while writing together is something that fills my heart in ways I cannot describe. I hope more people get to experience the type of contribution and friendship we share. Thank you! You are both amazing.

My professional career has been influenced so powerfully by these two incredible people. Mark Goldberg, thank you for always inspiring me to bring me best, be my best, and give my best to everyone around me. You've made me a better person. Mark Sorensen, I am so honored to have you in my life. You are truly a genuine man of integrity, compassion, and intellect, with a true passion for helping people in the investment management world. You truly live by the motto of "What you have done to improve the lives of your clients today?" I'm grateful for you.

More thanks to the people whom I feel are doing their best to improve the financial lives of pre-retirees and retirees. Tony Robbins, you are giving a larger platform to the message of fiduciary responsibility, we need to continue spreading the word. John "Jack" Bogle, Robert Kiyosaki, Dave Ramsey, Suze Orman, Ed Slott, Tom Skiff, Peter Gelbwaks you inspire me, through your professionalism and being "game-changers"

I'd like to give a heartfelt thank you to Vishen Lakhiani. Your vision and work inspires me to be true to myself and continue my path of self-improvement.

Jason Goldberg, you remind me that I sometimes have a terrible habit of taking life too seriously. I have a greater understanding of the value of "playful prosperity" because of you. "High five" buddy!

Zari Paristeh, you have shown me so much unconditional love and have contributed so much to the understanding of myself, others and our connection. I'm so grateful for our friendship and the time we spend together.

Last, I'd like to acknowledge the fact that this work is truly the result of the interactions I've had from everyone in my past. This work is living proof that we are all connected and benefit from sharing life together. This is my gift of gratitude back to you. We are all one. Love is my religion…

APPENDIX

There are many misconceptions and misunderstanding about the role of insurance and its importance in retirement planning. As we reviewed early, it's smart to use strategies from the securities *and* insurance world to build a strong retirement plan.

The following information are the top three strategies I consider when designing plans for my private clients. Sometimes, we use all of these strategies and sometimes we use just one strategy we are going to review.

What you use in your plan is influenced by two things.

#1 What your adviser believes is professionally suitable for you.

#2 Who are you?

It's my intention that the explanation of the strategies below provides a 30,000 foot snapshot of how strategies like this may fit in your plan and how they may benefit you.

ASSET PRESERVATION STRATEGIES

Annuities

Before we talk annuities, let me ask you a question. If there were a mutual fund available that allowed you to participate in most of the upside gains of an index and locked in your gains year after year, but didn't participate in market losses would you be interested? Uh… I would. Well, guess what? They do exist. I'll explain later in this section.

First, the annuity topic can be taboo in some circles. Truth be told, I hate most annuity plans. However, there are some very powerful and effective plans available. You just need to know what to look for.

Let me share with you the types of plans that are available and the criteria I use to analyze their effectiveness. Keep in mind, these are not specific recommendations for your needs. We don't know each other, but the proceeding information will provide you with enough knowledge to seek the help of a qualified professional in your area and give you a good understanding of what may or may not interest you.

I have used a particular type of annuity over the years that have protected my private clients assets, deposited into the plans, from stock market declines, deferred taxes, avoided probate, while creating guaranteed lifetime income (if the client needs it).

Types

There are three types of annuity plans available (fixed, variable, & fixed-index).

I'm not going to go into high detail, but I will give you a great over-view and deepen your understanding. These plans are much easier to understand than what the public is meant to believe. I do recommend you seek the counsel of an independent adviser who can help you decide what plan is right for your specific situation.

Here's what you need to know:

Annuities provide tax-deferral, probate avoidance, safety from stock market related losses and can create income for a lifetime. Unlike bank cd's many plans allow you to access your money with no penalties, in the case of a critical illness or need for qualified long term health care.

Fixed Annuities

Think of a fixed annuity as the insurance industries alternative to bank certificate of deposits (cd's). The insurance carriers are keenly aware they are competing with banks for guaranteed returns and typically offer a slightly higher rate than local banks.

People who typically use fixed annuities are the same people who turn to bank cd's for safety of principle in exchange for a small rate of return. These plans can be a better alternative to money market, savings, and checking accounts. Pretty simple stuff.

Variable Annuities

Variable annuities are nothing more than investment accounts with an insurance wrapper. A person who deposits money into a variable annuity would be able to choose from a menu of stocks, bonds, mutual funds, etc. to potentially grow their deposit. A prospectus is involved.

Here's the dirty little secret. Expense charges are much higher than a traditional brokerage account. The principle is typically not protected from investment choice losses, meaning it is possible to lose principle.

To make up for that, variable annuity insurers began offering lifetime income producing plans. These income producing accounts are merely accounting values and do not reflect actual cash values.

Buyer beware, it is possible to have a cash account balance less than the original deposit, while the income producing account is much higher. Here's how…

In order to downplay the potential for principle losses, the insurer and sales person will position the annuity as an income producing strategy and downplay the fact the plan has high fees and potential for losses in the cash value. Tricky huh? So pay attention. You want both, by the way.

Your cash value account will participate (up or down) with the performance of the strategies you elect from the prospectus and your income account may grow by a declared rate specified by the carrier. This interest rate could be a guaranteed 5% or 7% for example.

The guaranteed growth rate of the income producing account helps to predict what income may be in the future, depending on what age the person elects to collect income payments.

If a variable annuity is to be used solely to produce income, then why incur all of the high expenses related to the investment accounts? In my opinion, it makes no sense when we compare it to the next strategy.

Fixed Indexed Annuities

Fixed indexed annuities (FIA's) offer principle protection from stock market related losses and typically lock in contract gains each year, every two years, or every 5 years. This means that each time the gain is credited and locked in, you now have a new low and cannot have the new balance lost by stock market related losses. Some plans do have small fee's that could reduce the cash value, similar to low cost investments, but your principle is protected as I described above.

So how can you avoid principle reduction from stock market losses while being credited annual gains? It sounds too good to be true. I hear it all the time. Here's the truth.

FIA's will not credit gains equal to the S&P 500 or DJIA indices, although they are typically much higher than money market accounts, bank cd's, checking and savings accounts. Rather, they allow you to participate in most of the upside gains, while being protected from market related losses.

Do you remember my question at the beginning of this section? I don't know about you, but I'm o.k. receiving most of the gains of an index as long as I don't have to take any of the losses.

> Remember, one of the most important rules of investing:
> It's not what you make, but what you keep that counts!

FIA insurers are well aware of the lifetime income accounts offered by variable annuity competitors and offer much better growth and payouts for their income producing accounts. It's worth noting that FIA income accounts are the same as variable annuity income accounts. In the regard, they are both accounting values and not actual cash values.

So how can FIA's offer better performing lifetime income accounts compared to variable annuities? I'll give you something to think about.

Let's assume we have two companies, A & B. You deposit $100k of your money into company A plan. Inside the plan you buy stock, bonds and mutual funds. There are fees and maintenance charges, cost of insurance charges, and income account charges. They really add up!

Over the course of 5 years the plan does pretty well, but then 2008 happens…again. The market loses and loses bad. Guess what? So does the company A plan cash value. The cash value is not $100,000 5 years later. It's $80,000. $20,000 less than what you started with 5 years earlier.

You are fed up with taking losses and decide to take income. Just hang with me for a moment.

Now, let's look at company B. You deposit $100k into company B plan. You do not buy any stock, bonds or mutual funds. There are no fees and maintenance charges, or cost of insurance charge, but you do pay a fee for your income account. Over the course of 5 years, the plan grows for the first 4 and the gains are locked in each year. In the 5th year another 2008 happens. The market loses big, but the gains you locked in for the first four years are protected from market related losses.

You are fed up with the stock market, even though you didn't participate in the losses, and decide to take income.

Personal Strategy Session

In this example, who do you think can provide a higher lifetime income payout?

Would you believe company A, who has market exposure and losses on the books? Or company B, who has no market exposure without losses on the books? Yeah, I think company B would have the ability to pay a higher lifetime income. Do you know who company A and company B represent in this story?

You got it right. Company A is the variable annuity insurer and company B is the FIA insurer. So, if you are interested in creating an income stream you cannot outlive remember this example and choose wisely.

This is an important lesson and can help you protect your money from high fees in variable annuities and receive higher income in retirement. Who doesn't want that?

There is a common misconception that if you deposit money into a variable annuity or fixed index annuity the insurance company gets to keep your money. That is simply not true.

Your beneficiaries would receive the cash value of the plan minus any withdraws taken during the life of the plan. The money received from the income account will reduce the cash value account dollar for dollar. Makes sense, right?

Here's a few FYI's I believe everyone needs to be aware of. Make sure you consult a trained, experienced, independent adviser that will match your situation and goals with the insurer who will give you the most potential return, lowest fees, and most liquidity for your money.

Annuities can have surrender fees, if the contract is surrendered prior to the contract term. Please understand the specific annuity contract for the surrender fees, potential returns, fee schedules and liquidity provided by the insurer.

If structured properly with the rest of your portfolio, surrender fees should never be an issue (think of the "Bucket System" we talked about earlier). I recommend, you should always have, at least, 30% of your money liquid in other strategies in case of emergencies. When working with a trusted adviser, you should have identified how much money you would like to have in your 9 a.m. bucket, before you would ever put money inside of an annuity.

In my private practice, I've never had a client incur a surrender fee. I believe this is because the due diligence is done to address how an emergency would be funded. In other words, where would we get the money in case of an emergency? Could we pay for it with 9 a.m. money? Is it possible to withdraw money from a non-retirement investment account? Would it be best to take money from an IRA?

These are the questions you can ask yourself. One of the most important considerations when addressing this question, for me, is what is the most tax efficient way to solve the problem without affecting the strategy that produces income in retirement. We don't want to have any impact on that strategy.

Last thing about these plans, rates and contract terms can vary state to state.

Long Term Health Care Insurance

Long term health care costs pose the most dangerous threat to your retirement savings. Consider this, According to the U.S. Department of Health and Human Services, "At least 70 percent of people over age 65 will require some long-term care services at some point in their lives." (National Clearinghouse for LTC Information).

That's a staggering statistic. What's worse is, the average cost for a year of home health care is approximately $45,000 nationwide, according to Genworth Financials 2017 Annual Cost of Care Survey.

Even though odds are stacked against us that we will need some type of care after age 65, very few of us really believe something like this can happen to us individually. So let me ask you a few questions. Would you ever go without homeowners insurance? Would you ever do without auto insurance, even if it wasn't required? Consider this:

The National Academy of Elder Law Attorneys did a study comparing the risk of financial hardship caused by Long Term Health Care, with the risk of financial hardship caused by a major automobile accident or a house fire. Here's what they reported.

- Automobile Accident: **1 out of 240 [0.4%]**
- House Fire: **1 out of 1,200 [0.08%]**
- Long Term Care: **1 out of 2 [50%]**

THE "ONE MILLION DOLLAR" QUESTION

What is the "One Million Dollar" question? Simply, it's what everyone really wants to know when thinking about this topic. When is the right time to purchase a long-term health care insurance plan?

My best answer is the moment before you have a crisis that requires you *needing* long-term health care. Unfortunately, that requires a crystal ball. So, considering these plans are age and health rated, the best time to purchase a plan is now! Do not wait.

It has happened more times than I can count, a person or couple has delayed purchasing coverage because they thought they were too young or something like this would never happen to them. They have a health event like a heart attack, serious fall, car accident, cancer diagnosis, or stroke and now they want to get coverage, and I have to explain to them they are not eligible because of their health.

Don't be this person. Emotionally, it's hard to hear the pain, frustration and disappointment in their voices when I have to speak with these folks. Long term health care services are only getting more expensive every year, which makes long-term health care insurance more expensive every year you wait to apply.

Three criteria you must consider when deciding when is the right time to purchase a long-term health care insurance plan.

1. Plans are age rated. The younger you are, the more affordable your premiums will be. Premiums slowly climb throughout the 50 to 60-age band. They then climb faster in the early 60's. Premiums rise even faster from age 65 to 70, and they climb dramatically every year after age 70 a person waits to apply. Dramatically!

2. People typically don't get healthier as they age. By the time most people are in there mid to late 50s, they are taking some form of medication to treat things like depression, hypertension, arthritis, diabetes, osteoporosis, joint problems, etc. Each medication a person uses or health condition that is treated can be a reason for the insurance carrier to not award a preferred (most affordable) underwriting class. Health conditions don't have a date they magically happen. They happen unpredictably and to EVERYONE. You just never know when it's your time.

3. The cost of care grows every year with inflation. Very generally, the cost of care has risen around 4.5% the last 15 years. It's my opinion that they may rise faster in the coming years due to the laws of supply and demand. We have the largest demographic of our population (baby boomers) needing care in greater numbers every year. Most assisted living facilities and nursing care facilities have better than a 90% occupancy rate.

So, when is the right time to purchase a long-term care insurance plan? Taking into consideration potential health changes and the age ratings systems of the carriers… NOW is the best time to purchase coverage. Don't delay and cost yourself money and potentially lose the opportunity to get coverage due to a health event.

WHAT IS A TAX-QUALIFIED LTCI PLAN?

For federal tax purposes, tax-qualified (TQ) long-term care insurance is treated like accident and health insurance. TQ long-term care insurance premiums are considered to be a medical expense and qualify as an itemized deduction up to a defined limit, based on the age of the policyholder and inflation.

The younger you are, the less you can deduct. No benefits you receive will be taxed. This is a huge advantage. Non-reimbursed, long-term care services are also considered a medical expense and can be claimed as itemized deductions to the extent they exceed 7.5 percent of adjusted gross annual income. If you are the owner of a C-Corporation, it may be possible to write off your LTCi premiums as a business expense AND receive benefits tax-free. I always advise consulting a qualified tax advisory firm about your specific tax situation and long term care coverage.

Here's the really good part! Because the federal government is turning a "blind-eye" to this being a taxable event, they have defined how you qualify to get paid by ALL tax-qualified LTCi plans. So, what you are about to read is the same for every single carrier offering tax-qualified LTCi plans.

Qualifying for a claim to be paid is simple. All you need to do is have a health care professional (yours, not the insurance company's) certify that you need help with one of two things for a period of at least 90 days.

1) Help with two out of six activities of daily living (ADL) bathing, eating, dressing, using the bathroom, transferring or continence.

or

2) Require assistance within arm's reach because of a cognitive impairment such as Alzheimer's disease, dementia or spinal cord injury.

Let's focus on No.1 for a moment. It's possible that an insured could temporarily receive benefits because of an injury or surgery, recover, discontinue receiving claim benefits and go back to living a normal healthy life. Meanwhile, the insured still has benefits to use at another point in time. You can turn these plans on and off throughout your entire lifetime. It's not a use it or lose it account and you can turn this on and off throughout your life.

WHAT IS A PARTNERSHIP QUALIFIED LONG-TERM CARE INSURANCE PLAN?

If you are considering a long-term care insurance (LTCi) plan to protect your asset from the high cost of long-term health care, you owe it to yourself to understand the power of a Partnership qualified plan. Partnership approved plans are designated as tax-qualified and have a minimum level of benefits required to be in the plan.

All LTCi agents and advisers must complete a special training program to offer LTCi Partnership approved plans. The training is required to ensure each agent/adviser understands Partnership approved LTCi plans and how to correctly design the plans to qualify for the Partnership standards.

> I recommend when you are researching the market and getting quotes for coverage to specifically request a Partnership approved plan. Any experienced and trusted adviser you work with should be automatically recommending coverage that satisfies the Partnership standards. There is no extra cost of having a Partnership plan and the benefits are tremendous, in my opinion.

Later in the chapter, I talk about legacy planning. Well, if you are this type of person, you're going to really like what you're about to read. Partnership qualified plans allow you to protect the same amount of personal liquid assets that you would receive from your LTCi plan from Medicaid spend down. Confusing? It's really not.

Generally speaking, most of us understand that in order to qualify for Medicaid you cannot have more than $2000 of personal assets, not including your primary home or vehicle, and you can only retain $500k of home equity. Additionally, you will be required to submit your previous five years of financial records to prove you have not gifted assets away to impoverish yourself. This makes it very difficult for many families to qualify for Medicaid.

Now for the magic sauce! If you own a Partnership qualified LTCi plan, you can protect a significant portion of your assets (if not all) from Medicaid spend down. This allows you to pass more of your assets to your healthy spouse, kids, grandkids, favorite church, or charity.

> Here's how it works. For every dollar you receive from your LTCi plan, you can protect a dollar of your own personal liquid assets from spend down.

Here's an example: If you had exhausted your LTCi plan after receiving $350K in paid benefits, to you from your LTCi plan, and still need care, you can qualify for Medicaid, and you are allowed to shield and retain the same $350K of personal assets for the benefit of your healthy spouse, family, church or charity. In my opinion, this truly doubles the amount of asset protection in your LTCi plan. That's the magic sauce, and you pay no extra for it.

I believe this is an incredible benefit for families. Families are now able to pass more assets to their heirs, which is very important in today's economic situation. Young families need both parents working to make ends meet and are having more difficulty meeting their own savings goals.

Rather than spending a family's life savings on long-term health care and giving it away to the wealthy owner or corporation of a long-term health care facility, you can have a better chance of keeping your hard saved money in the family. A gift in the form of a financial legacy can be an incredible gift to your family. Having a Partnership qualified plan helps to ensure you are able to pass more, rather than less, to your family if you need help with long-term health care.

WHAT DO THESE PLANS COVER?

Most people believe LTCi is difficult to understand and that policies range widely with what is covered. In my opinion, nothing could be further from the truth. After reading this chapter, you will learn LTCi is far easier to understand compared to what the public is lead to believe.

As a standard feature, tax-qualified Partnership approved plans cover custodial care received in the following places and methods:

- Your own home
- Adult daycare center
- Assisted living facility
- Nursing care facility
- Hospice care
- Respite care

WHAT DO THESE PLANS NOT COVER?

Now this could be a much longer list, but I'll put it in easy terms for us all to understand. Anything that your short-term medical insurance will cover is what long-term care insurance will not cover. Here is a short list of what your medical insurance will cover:

- Doctor office visits
- Prescription drugs
- Surgery
- Medical testing
- X-rays

Remember, LTCi is defined as custodial care, which is typically NOT covered by short-term medical insurance. That's why LTCi was designed — to pay for what medical insurance does not pay for. It's really that simple.

WHAT TYPE OF LEGACY PLANNER ARE YOU?

Long-term care health care insurance is an asset protection device. Therefore, it is widely used as an estate protection tool. The amount of long-term health care coverage you use largely is influenced by what type of legacy planner you are.

There are typically two types of legacy planners.

1. Someone with the desire to leave assets for the benefit of children, grandchildren, favorite church, or charity. These planners should be using a plan to protect their assets for the benefit of their legacy beneficiaries. I typically recommend 70% - 90% coverage. This will help ensure a legacy is properly executed and family members, church and/or charity will be able to fully benefit from the deceased's generosity.

2. Someone with little or no desire to leave assets for the benefit of children, grandchildren, favorite church or charity – The largest concern is not running out of money for the long-term health care needs and impoverishing a healthy spouse or being a financial burden to family or being a financial ward of the State dependent on Medicaid.

These planners are usually more open to using more of their own money to solve the problem and typically more comfortable with a plan paying 50%-

70% of the cost of care. These legacy planners are more open to catastrophic plans to cover catastrophic financial hardship.

It is possible for spouses/partners to have different ideas about legacy planning. That's why it's important to address the topic.

Your legacy plan is one of the most important ways to take control of how to build a LTCi plan that will add strength and synergy to your overall retirement plan without over or under-insuring your family! It amazes me how most salespeople are not trained to even consider a family's legacy plan for long-term health care planning.

Seek the help of a long-term care insurance specialist for help designing and finding the best coverage specific to your situation.

Properly designed LTCi coverage is more affordable than you think. It's amazing to me the amount of people who bring quotes to my office, for me to review, that are improperly designed and cost far too much. They are frustrated at the potential costs, but relieved when they discover comprehensive coverage is much more affordable when properly designed.

Please keep in mind, some coverage is better than going without coverage. You don't need to have a plan that pays for everything.

Life Insurance

One of the most powerful ways to multiply your money in retirement is with life insurance. If you are the type of person who has a desire to leave money as a legacy, you should seriously consider life insurance. Many wealthy families ensure a healthy legacy is passed to heirs (family, charity, religious, academic) using this strategy.

There is a big misunderstanding in the population regarding the benefits of these plans. I could dedicate pages to this topic, but I'm going to give you the high points of some of the advantages I see in life insurance for most people near or in retirement.

Each type of life insurance has its advantages for the right person. The trick is to know which is best for you. Here's a quick guide to help you begin the process of understanding how each type might work for you.

Term Life Insurance

Most of us know term life insurance only lasts for a defined period of time. During that time frame we are able to benefit from the most life insurance coverage for the "cheapest" premium (price) and the rates are guaranteed not to change during that defined period of time. However, once the defined coverage period is over, you will see the rates increase *dramatically*.

Not to worry. You are not required to continue to pay the new premiums. I advise my private clients to re-shop plans and new rates, if they would like to continue being covered.

I like to think term life insurance serves two purposes for clients I serve.

#1 Term life coverage is great at providing a surviving spouse and/or family members a tax-free death benefit that can be used to pay off debt (i.e. mortgage, credit cards, auto loans, you name it).

#2 Term life coverage is a very affordable way to provide a significant benefit to a surviving spouse to help them maintain the lifestyle they are accustomed to. This may be especially true for a couple who have chosen a single life pension payout. Single life pension payouts typically cease paying when the covered person passes, leaving the surviving spouse without the income they may be accustomed to.

In my experience, most people's debt decreases as they age. The mortgage may be paid off and credit cards debt is usually a minimum. So, I typically see term life insurance as a decreasing need as people age.

Permanent Life Insurance

Permanent life insurance provides lifetime coverage. There are two types: whole life and universal life. Each type of plan has two parts: life insurance and saving/investment options.

Both of these plans can be used to provide a tax-deferred growth strategy for money not in a qualified retirement plan. Premiums are much higher than term life insurance. I'll explain why.

Premiums are higher because of the two parts I mentioned above. Unlike term life insurance, which provides no cash value, permanent life insurance provides a death benefit AND the potential to grow your cash. Think of it as an investment account with a life insurance wrapper.

There are two important terms for you to know. They are very simple, but because they sound alike, it's easy to mix them up.

> Face value = The amount of life insurance in the policy PLUS the amount of cash you have accumulated in the policy. These, in combination, are what would be gifted tax-free to heirs.
>
> Cash value = The accumulated value of your deposits plus interest. This is the value the insurance company would use to determine the amount of loan you may be able to take against the policy, if needed.

In your cash value account, a portion of your dollars are invested, as you direct, by the insurance company to grow the cash that you are funding the plan with (minus the cost of the insurance expense). So…your cash has the ability to grow in coordination with the strategy you select. One of the common thoughts about this strategy is that there is no access to the money deposited into the plan.

In fact, you do have access in the form of policy loans. One of the benefits of policy loans from permanent life insurance is that loan rates are typically lower than other market rates. If you are not able to pay back the loan, the company would simply deduct the loan balance from the cash value that has accumulated in the plan. Warning: I recommend you only borrow what you intend to pay back.

These are the most basic and important facts you need to know about these plans. We could literally write another book just on life insurance, but the information I shared with you, and what I will share next, provides a great base of understanding to get the discussion started.

Whole Life Insurance vs Universal Life Insurance

Whole Life Insurance

Whole life insurance is designed as an alternative long-term savings plan and it is important to keep the policy as long as you live. The younger you start the more affordable your premiums are long term. Premiums are fixed and do not change for the life of the policy. You are expected to pay premiums for the length of time you elect when you begin the plan.

The insurer puts your money to work in a high interest savings account. If there is a surplus in earnings you may be able to elect to collect dividends or have them reinvested into your cash value account.

A few advantages of these plans are you can take a policy loan and have the potential to earn dividend payments from the insurer. They are great for the long-term saver because the money grows tax-deferred and can help provide income to surviving spouses and pay for post-death expenses.

Universal Life Insurance

In general, universal life insurance offers more flexibility than whole life and you can even think of it as "adjustable life insurance", if that helps your understanding. After your policy is issued and you have paid the first premium most insurers will allow you to increase or decrease your premiums and death benefit.

This is useful if your finances get tight. If finances were really tight you could suspend premium payments and allow them to be paid with the cash value of the policy. Beware that this strategy will reduce your cash value, affecting the cash value *AND* the face value downward.

It's fair to review the two types of universal life insurance. There is "Traditional" Universal life insurance and "Indexed" Universal life insurance (IUL). In very broad terms, here's a simple way to distinguish them from each other. Think of "traditional" to be similar to whole life insurance, with the additional benefits listed above, and "index" to be similar to "fixed-indexed" annuities.

From there you have a pretty good understanding of some of positives and negatives of both. The advantage over annuities is the obvious multiplication of your money by the addition of life insurance. However, if you are not insurable, a life plan is not an option for you.

"Traditional" plans give you the opportunity to earn good rates of return, and collect dividend payments. As a wealth transfer strategy, these policies get the job done. When used in an irrevocable life insurance trust, premiums can be more affordable than other life strategies because the death benefit rather than the cash value matters.

IUL's are a bit more costly that "traditional" plans, but less expensive than whole life insurance. Similar to the annuity cousins, IUL's are not subject to the risk of market related losses. This is a potentially big advantage for a person who likes the potential for higher returns, in the cash value, with no opportunity for loss.

In closing, life insurance is a fantastic way to multiply your money in retirement. You may use one "type" of plan and you may use all three types. It's worth consideration while you are at your current age and in good health.

As I said, my commentary is intended to help you begin thinking about how these strategies might work for you and the advantages of each. I consider this the 30,000' view. I encourage you to seek the help of a qualified independent life insurance adviser to tailor make a plan that adds strength and synergy to what you are currently doing and where you want to be.

Now go shape the life you've been delaying for decades. Go!!!

~Squeeze the most out of life with ease and fun~

BIBLIOGRAPHY

Chapter 3

[1] Wall Street Journal February 1, 2010 Shift From Commissions to Fees Has Benefits For Fund Investors, Karen Damato and Jaime Levy Pessin

[2] Wall Street Journal March 28, 2009, The Fight Over Who Will Guard Your Nest Egg, Jason Zweig

Chapter 6
[3] http://www.bronnieware.com/blog/regrets-of-the-dying

Chapter 9

[4] National Center for Health Statistics, National Vital Statistics Reports. Web:www.cdc.gov/nchs.

Chapter 14

[5] www.ThePassionTest.com

Chapter 21

[6] www.herox.com

[7] www.gofundme.com

[8] www.kiva.org

[9] http://www.water4.org/fightfortheforgotten

[10] www.changeheroes.com

[11] www.travelingspoon.com

[12] www.imermanangels.org

[13] www.guitarcenter.com

[14] www.youtube.com

[15] National Association of Certified Mediators:
http://www.mediatorcertification.org/

[16] https://www.grantprofessionals.org/

[17] www.meetup.com

[18] www.retirementdreammaker.com